SpringerBriefs in Law

For further volumes:
http://www.springer.com/series/10164

Jonathan Herring

Relational Autonomy and Family Law

Springer

Jonathan Herring
Exeter College
University of Oxford
Oxford
UK

ISSN 2192-855X ISSN 2192-8568 (electronic)
ISBN 978-3-319-04986-1 ISBN 978-3-319-04987-8 (eBook)
DOI 10.1007/978-3-319-04987-8
Springer Cham Heidelberg New York Dordrecht London

Library of Congress Control Number: 2014934678

Printed on acid-free paper

Springer is part of Springer Science+Business Media (www.springer.com)

Contents

Abstract

This book explores the importance of autonomy in family law.[1] It argues that traditional understandings of autonomy are inappropriate in the family law context and instead recommends the use of relational autonomy. The book will start by explaining how autonomy has historically been understood, before exploring the problems with its use in family law. It will then set out the model of relational autonomy which, it will be argued, is more appropriate in this context. Finally, some examples of practical application will be presented. While the book will use examples from English law, the issues raised and theoretical discussion are relevant to any jurisdiction.

[1] This draws from previous work including Herring (2010) and Herring (2009).

Chapter 1
The Meaning of Autonomy

At its heart autonomy, traditionally understood, involves a claim that individuals should be allowed to make decisions for themselves and that those decisions should be respected by others, unless the decision involves harming someone else. Raz (1986, p. 369) defines it in this way:

> The ruling idea behind the ideal of personal autonomy is that people should make their own lives. The autonomous person is a (part) author of his own life. The ideal of personal autonomy is the vision of people controlling, to some degree, their own destiny, fashioning it through successive decisions throughout their lives.

Such an understanding of autonomy is central to a liberal conception of the self. Reece (2003, p. 13) explains:

> within liberalism, what is arguably most essential to the individual's identity is the individual's capacity to choose his or her own roles and identities, and to rethink those choices.

This individualist conception of autonomy is linked to a whole set of other values: self-sufficiency, self-sovereignty, moral independence, self-government, pluralism and liberty (Fineman 2004, Chap. 1). The freedom to able to make decisions as to how you live your life is seen a central part of 'Western political culture' (Dworkin 1993, p. 166). Alghrani and Harris (2006, p. 192) have claimed that:

> one of the presumption of liberal democracies is that the freedom of citizens should not be interfered with unless good and sufficient justification can be produced for so doing… The presumption is that citizens should be free to make their own choices in the light of their own values, whether or not these choices and values are acceptable to the majority. Only serious danger, either to other citizens or society, is sufficient to rebut this presumption.

So understood, autonomy is one of the most important rights an individual has (Griffin 2007, Chap. 1). Indeed it might even be seen as the source of all rights. Without autonomy we cannot choose how to exercise our other rights and they become worthless or, even worse, tools that others can use against us.

J. Herring, *Relational Autonomy and Family Law*, SpringerBriefs in Law,
DOI: 10.1007/978-3-319-04987-8_1,

Autonomy has achieved a 'sacred status' (Chen-Wishart 2007, p. 221) in legal writing and within wider social discourse. The themes of independence, self-determination and choice play a major role in public debates and popular culture. Politicians urge us to be self-supporting and free from reliance on the state; policies for disabled people are designed to enable independence; and there is strong condemnation of the "nanny state" telling us what to do. Many of the fictional heroes of our day: Jack Bauer, James Bond, Jason Bourne fight alone against the wicked powers that be: they are the epitome of the isolated autonomous man. The absence of autonomy is seen as something to dread. Ninety-three per cent of those seeking assisted dying in Oregon cited "loss of autonomy" as the reason they wished to die (Oregon Public Health Division 2013, p. 3). Independence and freedom have become the icons of our age. Yet, it will be argued, in the context of family law these are false gods.

The significance of autonomy is reflected in legal structures. A central role of the law is to seen as protecting individuals' autonomy from invasion from the state or from others. The rights attached to individualistic autonomy are concerned with fighting off unwanted intrusions into a person's freedom of choice (Donchin 2001, p. 188). Hence the criminal law protects bodies from unwanted touches and property law protects our goods from unwanted interference. Justice Brandeis, dissenting, in *Olmstead v. United States* (1928) has identified the 'right to be let alone' as the most valuable right belonging to 'civilized men'. Not only that but autonomy explains why people can be held to account for their actions. They have the choice to act in the way they do and so are responsible for the decisions they make.

Bridgeman (2007, p. 11), before criticising the concept, explains the law's response to individualistic autonomy in this way:

> all individuals exercise their autonomy and pursue their own ends within the shadow of the possibility of conflict arising from a clash of interests individually desired. Criminal and civil laws place limits upon the selfish pursuit of individual interest and seek to protect the individual from invasion of the boundaries of their bodies.

So seen, a central purpose of the law is to leave individuals free to pursue their autonomy, while providing means to resolve disputes when individuals' rights clash. Hence Article 8 of the European Convention of Human Rights, which protects, *inter alia*, the right to respect for private life, has been interpreted to protect autonomy. In *Ternovszky v. Hungary* (2009), para 22 the European Court of Human Rights were explicit about this:

> The notion of personal autonomy is a fundamental principle underlying the interpretation of the guarantees of Article 8.

Central to most understandings of autonomy is that a person's decision must be respected, even if it is regarded as foolish. This is captured in England's Mental Capacity Act 2005, which, in Section 1(4), states:

> A person is not to be treated as unable to make a decision merely because he makes an unwise decision.

At most we might discourage our friends from making a foolish decision, but ultimately the decision is one for them alone. That is because they that will bear the consequences, not us, and know themselves better than anyone else. And on many issues we have no better way of knowing what is best for them. Autonomy involves, therefore, a strong rejection of paternalism. With paternalism the state, or individual, imposes their views on another, based on an assessment of that person's best interests. That, it is said, denies people their "moral status as persons" (Ho 2008, p. 193). It treats the person as an object to be used to peruse the decision-makers version of what makes a good life.

At a broader political level support for autonomy encourages diversity, which is widely thought beneficial for a society. If the government allows individuals to develop their own ideas on religion and morality; and permits citizens to determine for themselves what is a good way to spend their time and money; and leaves people free to determine what friendships and community groups they wish to form this creates a pluralistic society, which is better in social and economic terms.

References

Alghrani A, Harris J (2006) Reproductive liberty: should the foundation of families be regulated? Child Family Law Q 18:191–211
Bridgeman J (2007) Parents, young children and healthcare law. Cambridge University Press, Cambridge
Chen-Wishart M (2007) Undue influence: vindicating relationships of influence. In: Holder J, O'Cinneide M (eds) Current legal problems. Oxford University Press, Oxford, pp 231–261
Donchin A (2001) Understanding autonomy relationally. J Med Philos 26:365–386
Dworkin R (1993) Life's dominion. Harper Collins, London
Fineman M (2004) The autonomy myth. New Press, New York
Griffin J (2007) On human rights. Oxford University Press, Oxford
Ho A (2008) The individualist model of autonomy and the challenge of disability. Bioethical Inq 5:193–207
Oregon Public Health Division (2013) Oregon's Death with Dignity Act—2012. Oregon Public Health Division, Ottawa
Raz J (1986) The morality of freedom. Oxford University Press, Oxford
Reece H (2003) Divorcing responsibly. Hart Publishing, Oxford

Chapter 2
Family Law and Autonomy

This section will argue that autonomy has come to play an increasing role in family law in recent decades. Traditionally autonomy was little discussed in family law. That was not surprising. It fits uncomfortably with what are commonly thought to be the central themes of family law: the responsibilities of parents; the state interest in upholding marriage; the establishment of blood ties; and the enforcement of obligations between spouses. None of these are readily reconcilable with the freedom to forge one's life story, which is at the heart of individualist models of autonomy. Yet in the past few decades the influence of autonomy on family law has been considerable. Here are two examples.

2.1 No Fault Divorce

Many of the arguments in favour of no fault or liberalised divorce were based on autonomy or self-determination. If both parties to a marriage wanted the marriage to come to an end then they should be free to pursue their own plans. It was argued that couples should not be prevented from divorcing based on some supposed moral principle. As Schneider (1994, p. 503) puts it:

> The duty of personal growth toward self-fulfilment and the imperative of autonomy crucially alter the modern morality of marriage. In particular, permanence can no longer be a principal marital ideal, for no relationship should persist that does not promote its true end-personal fulfilment. Since the search for fulfilment demands probing and developing one's identity and responding flexibly to one's discoveries, people are likely to change, sometimes becoming unsuitable partners in the quest for selfhood.

The move towards no fault divorce law reflected broader sociological understandings of relationships, particularly the concept of the "pure relationship" which Giddens (1992, p. 58) explains:

> refers to a situation where a social relation is entered into for its own sake, for what can be derived by each person from a sustained association with another; and which is continued only in so far as it is thought by both parties to deliver enough satisfaction for each individual to stay within it.

J. Herring, *Relational Autonomy and Family Law*, SpringerBriefs in Law,
DOI: 10.1007/978-3-319-04987-8_2,

So seen relationships are mere tools we use to develop "the reflexive narrative of the self" (Giddens 1992, p. 75). They are means to the end of self-satisfaction and if they are failing to achieve that goal they should be set aside. As we shall see later that understanding of relationships has received sustained criticism. Nevertheless it is very much in tune with notions of individualistic autonomy.

The notion of the pure relationship is commonly regarded as a potent example of a broader notion of individualism (Daly and Scheiwe 2010), where people seek to peruse their good life, and involve others only in so far as that is necessary. The ties and responsibilities of the old order, based on marriage and formal social roles, can be set aside to liberate the individual to set their own path (Beck and Beck-Gernsheim 2001; Beck-Gernsheim 2013). The growth of individualism has combined with economic developments, increasing standards of living, enabling people to be more self-reliant; more egalitarian views on gender roles; and higher aspirations for life, to produce a more fluid understanding of relationships. For women especially increased participation in the work force opened up a range of lifestyle options which had previously been closed off (Amato and Boyd 2013) and made divorce a social and economic, as well as legal, reality. No-fault divorce and rising divorce rates are commonly cited as symptoms of this increased individualism, which is closely tied to traditional understandings of autonomy.

2.2 Increased Use of Mediation

A second notable development has been the move towards increased use of mediation in family law disputes. Couples are increasingly encouraged to resolve disputes themselves, rather than using lawyers or the courts to find the solution. This is commonly justified using autonomy-based language. For example, England's Family Justice Review (Norgrave 2011, para 104), in the context of disputes over children, stated:

> Generally it seems better that parents resolve things for themselves if they can. They are then more likely to come to an understanding that will allow arrangements to change as they and their children change. Most people could do with better information to help this happen. Others need to be helped to find routes to resolve their disputes short of court proceedings.

The language of empowerment is used too. A Government White Paper (Department of Work and Pensions 2007, para 32) declares:

> We want to move to a child maintenance system that promotes greater parental responsibility and enables and empowers parents to make their own arrangements for child maintenance.

As these quotes suggests the role of family law shifts away from providing a framework for parties to negotiate a solution to their dispute (or occasionally imposes solutions) and instead the law's role is limited to assisting the parties to reach an agreement. It is for them, exercising their autonomy, to reach a solution in the terms they think is appropriate.

Reece (2000, p. 66) has written of the emphasis on the "responsible post-liberal" individual as at the heart of the proposed reforms to the Family Law Act 1996. Her observations are just as pertinent to some more recent legislation, such as the Children and Adoption Act 2006. She explains:

> The responsible post-liberal individual is judged, not by what he does but by how profoundly he has thought about what he does. The old view of responsibility was clear-cut; there just were certain actions that you should or should not take: "good behaviour is simple. It is about easy things. The choice may be difficult but the distinction is easy. Stealing is wrong; lying is wrong; telling the truth is right." The new form of responsibility is no longer about discrete decisions—responsible behaviour has shifted to a way of being, a mode of thought. Faced with the decision whether to tell a lie, we can no longer say with confidence that the responsible individual is the one who tells the truth. Now, the individual shows his responsibility by the attitude with which he approaches the decision, the extent to which he reflects on the implications of what he chooses.

This kind of thinking can be seen in the Government's recent proposals that an information hub be provided to help parents reach their own decisions:

> We propose that separating couples should go first to an information hub to give them ready access to a wide range of information and direction to further support as appropriate. This should emphasise shared parental responsibility throughout. The hub should:
>
> - focus parents to consider the needs of their child first, emphasising that a child will benefit from a continued relationship with both parents, where this is safe;
> - support parents to resolve their issues independently;
> - direct them to find available support to resolve any disputes outside of court; and help them to understand what to do and what to expect where an application to court is necessary.

So autonomy plays a central role: this is your decision and you must make it; but the government may offer advice and encouragement to help you make the decision and enable you to make a good decision. But ultimately the decision is yours. This approach regards family disputes as private matters which should be left for the couple to resolve, with the law's role being restricted to enable and encourage the couple to reach an agreement which is most appropriate for them. The reasons for this shift towards autonomous decision making are complex, but I suggest they include the following.

First, it fits in well with the Government's continued attempts to reduce expenditure. There have severe cut backs to the legal aid budget, particularly as it relates to family matters (Macdonald 2007; Eekelaar 2013). While the restrictions in legal aid provision are clearly in part motivated by a desire to cut government costs, they can conveniently be tied in with autonomy-based language. External values are not imposed by others, be that through legal advice or oversight of negotiations or judicial order in a court hearing. Couples are encouraged to resolve their family disputes themselves through mediation, creating their own solutions, which work for them, rather than involve expensive lawyers and the courts (Department of Work and Pensions 2011, p. 2). When combined with references to the greed of lawyers, the harsh restrictions on legal aid have been achieved with little objection from the general public.

Second, the Government is feeling the heat from complaints about the way courts and state bodies make decisions in relation to family matters. This is true particularly of the court's response to applications by non-resident fathers for contact with their children; concerns over child protection interventions; and complaints about the operation of the Child Support Agency. There is an understandable wish for Government to put to one side the political flak that can emanate from these controversial issues. The vocal campaigns of men's pressure groups in these areas have embarrassed the Government and courts. The response has involved attempts to shift decision making away from state agencies or courts and towards the couples themselves (Adoption and Children Act 2002; Child Maintenance and Other Payments Act 2008). These render the decisions less susceptible to public scrutiny and less likely to cause criticism of the Government.

Third, it has become common to claim that family disputes are essentially private disputes that matter only to the couple themselves. This can be seen in the increased use of mediation and the encouragement to use parenting plans. The Family Justice Review (Norgrave 2011, Annex A) states:

> The court's role should be focused on protecting the vulnerable from abuse, victimisation and exploitation and should avoid intervening in family life except where there is clear benefit to children or vulnerable adults in doing so.
> Individuals should have the right information and support to enable them to take responsibility for the consequences of their relationship breakdown.

This minimalist role for family courts may reflect a human rights era with an emphasis on respect for private life. In particular there is a general distrust of the state's interference in private and sexual matters. Eekelaar (2007, p. 82) has written powerfully of the need for the law to respect the 'a sphere of personal interaction' by not regulating the intimate aspects of life. There is some suggestion of this in the Government's argument explaining why legal aid should generally not be available in family law cases:

> there is a range of other cases which can very often result from a litigant's own decisions in their personal life... Where the issue is one which arises from the litigant's own personal choices, we are less likely to consider that these cases concern issues of the highest importance (Ministry of Justice 2010, para 4.19).

The next chapter will explore the difficulties in using traditional individualized autonomy in the family law context and explore how relational autonomy provides a more appropriate conceptual approach.

References

Amato P, Boyd L (2013) Children and divorce in world perspective. In: Abela A, Walker J (eds) Contemporary issues in family studies. Wiley Blackwell, Oxford
Beck U, Beck-Gernsheim E (2001) Individualisation. Sage, Thousand Oaks CA
Beck-Gernsheim (2013) From rights and obligations to contested rights and obligations: individualization, globalization, and family law. Theor Inq Law 13:1–14
Daly M, Scheiwe K (2010) Individualisation and personal obligations—social policy, family policy and law reform in Germany and the UK. Int J Law Policy Fam 24:177–197
Department of Work and Pensions (2007) A new system of child maintenance. Department of Work and Pensions, London
Department of Work and Pensions (2011) Strengthening families, promoting parental responsibility: the future of child maintenance (Cmd. 7990). The Stationery Office, London
Eekelaar J (2007) Family law and personal life. Oxford University Press, Oxford
Eekelaar J (2013) Then and now—family law's direction of travel. J Soc Welfare Fam Law 35:415–426
Giddens A (1992) Transformation of intimacy. Polity Press, Cambridge
Macdonald A (2007) Legal aid reform—beyond no more money. Fam Law 37:130–134
Ministry of Justice (2010) Proposals for the reform of legal aid in England and Wales, consultation paper CP 12/10. The Stationary Office, London
Norgrave D (2011) Family justice review. Ministry of Justice, London
Reece H (2000) Divorcing responsibly. Feminist Legal Stud 8:65–91
Schneider C (1994) Marriage, morals and the law: no-fault divorce and moral discourse. Utah Law Rev 503–585

Chapter 3
Relational Autonomy

The concept of relational autonomy is a response to the traditional individualised concept of autonomy. MacKenzie and Stoljar (2000, p. 4), two leading proponents of the concept, characterise it in these terms:

> ''relational autonomy'' is an umbrella term, designating a range of related perspectives...premised on a shared conviction that persons are socially embedded, that agents' identities are formed within the context of social relationships and shaped by a complex of intersecting social determinants, such as race, class, gender, and ethnicity.

It is based on a reconfiguration of the concept of autonomy (Herring 2009). Code (1991, p. 78) argues that for supporters of individualized autonomy:

> Autonomous man is—and should be—self-sufficient, independent, and self-reliant, a self-realizing individual who directs his efforts towards maximizing his personal gains. His independence is under constant threat from other (equally self-serving) individuals: hence he devises rules to protect himself from intrusion. Talk of right, rational self-interest, expedience, and efficiency permeates his moral, social, and political discourse. In short, there has been a gradual alignment of autonomy with individualism.

Relational autonomy supporters firmly reject such an analysis. The following are some of the key themes in writings on relational autonomy.

3.1 Relational Life Inevitable

The starting point for an approach based on relational autonomy is that a relational life is inevitable. From our earliest days are character and understanding of ourselves is fixed by our relationships with others (Carle 2005, p. 307). We all at some points in our lives have been dependent on others for our survival and many people others are dependent on us (Sanders 2013, p. 2). For many people their self-definition of themselves is based on relationship. Nedelsky (2012, p. 1) writes:

> Relationships are central to people's lives—to who we are, to the capacities we are able to develop, to what we value, what we suffer, and what we are able to enjoy.

J. Herring, *Relational Autonomy and Family Law*, SpringerBriefs in Law,
DOI: 10.1007/978-3-319-04987-8_3,

For many their self-definition is based on relationship (Barvosa-Carter 2007, p. 19), be it as friend, flautist or Fulham Football Club fan. Our sense of self is a mixture of interlocking and sometimes conflicting social identities (Donchin 2000, p. 188; Mackenzie 2008). We are not in reality free to "live our lives as we choose" because we are constrained by the responsibilities, realities and relationships which embed our lives (Nedelsky 1989, p. 343). Hence Johnson (1997, p. 30) has called our culture's insistence that we are separate and autonomous as patriarchy's 'Great Lie'. Judicial recognition for this can be found too. Justice Sachs in National Coalition for Gay and Lesbian Equality v Minister of Justice (1999, para 117) stated:

> While recognising the unique worth of each person, the Constitution does not presuppose that a holder of rights is an isolated, lonely and abstract figure possessing a disembodied and socially disconnected self. It acknowledges that people live in their bodies, their communities, their cultures, their places and their times.

Autonomous choice can only be found by sharing our ideas, aspirations and hopes with others (Barclay 2000). Further, our decisions are not just 'ours' they usually affect those we are in relationship and their decisions will affect us. As Slife and Richardson (2011, p. 304) put it:

> we do not, indeed cannot, construct meanings to live by on our own, individualistically, without sensitively and responsibly coordinating our action, reflection, and creative imagination with that of other people.

Indeed Kenneth Gergen has gone even further and argued that it is only through relationships that the self exists. He talks of the co-construction of the self with others (Gergen 2009, p. 12). His argument is more radical than some relational theorists who argue that we find our identity and meaning through relationships. He (Gergen 2011, p. 13) argues:

> It is not individuals who come together to form relationships; rather, it is out of collaborative action (or co-action) that the very conception of the individual mind comes into existence (or not). On this view, psychological processes such as thinking and feeling do not precede (or cause) our actions. Rather, all intelligible actions are relational in origin and performance. We do not possess emotions independent of relationships, for example. Rather, it is because we participate in relational traditions that we recognize ourselves as having emotions and that we navigate when, where, and how they can be performed.

In particular, family life is not about separation and self-sufficiency. It is about pooling talents and resources to work together for the good of the family (Baker 2011). Rather than the value of independency being key, it is values of trust, care and intimacy which are central (Verkerk 2001). Our autonomy (our wishes for our lives) can only be performed and can only be understood by reference to our relationships (Verkerk 2001, p. 290). A good example of this comes from a study on leisure time activities of parents in the USA by Shaw (2008, pp. 6–9) which found:

> Many parents…place emphasis on…children learning about 'the family' as a value and the importance of family togetherness. In this sense, the purpose of family leisure is not simply something that is done for the sake of the children and/or to enhance child

> development, but also *for the sake of the family as a whole and for shared family ideas and family cohesion*... Family leisure is seen as a way to 'cement' relationships and *ensure the stability of the family unit.*

Ribbens McCarthy (2012, p. 85) writes of her interviews with many people:

> Themes of family as a supportive unit stretching backwards and forwards in time, providing a sense of belonging and care, and evoking deep emotions, are thus highly pervasive in the studies I have been considering here, even against lived experiences that are strongly at odds with such a view.

She goes on (at 86) to outline the idea of a "relational individual":

> an entity that is produced through, and continually embedded in, relationships, but experienced as a (largely self-directing) individual; well-being is bound up with the web of relationships to which the person belongs but care of (the unique) 'self' is also important.

All of this challenges the notions of self, chosen goals, and pursuing one's vision for the good life, which is at the heart of the individualised conception of autonomy. Indeed, these are all powerful reasons to question to the individualism which is said to permeate modern society. Clearly people do value their relationships greatly and do not see life as simply about perusing one's own goals (Smart 2007; Eekelaar 2013). Glendon (1989, p. 112) writes:

> [T]he legal imagery of separateness and independence [in U.S. family law] contrasts everywhere with the way most functioning families operate and with the circumstances of mothers and young children in both intact and broken homes. Yet the law holds self-sufficiency up as an ideal, suggesting that dependency is somehow degrading, and implicitly denying the importance of human inter-subjectivity.

As already mentioned, for traditional autonomy the law's role is enable people to be free from outside interference, to only be subject to those obligations they have chosen to undertake. Becker (1999, p. 21) writes: "patriarchy values power, control, autonomy, independence, toughness, invulnerability, strength, aggressiveness, rationality, detachment (being non-emotional), and other traditionally masculine attributes that have proven effective in the battle against other men." These values are rejected by relational approaches. Rather people are understood as relational, interconnected and interdependent. The law's job is to uphold and maintain relationships and protect people from the abuses that can occur within them.

It is for these reason that there has been criticism of Antony Giddens' argument in favour of the "pure relationship" mentioned earlier. Mulinari and Sandell (2009, p. 494) argue that it abstracted and dissociated from every day life. The notion of relationships being used as part of a project of self-development and disposed of if failing to fulfil that role, makes no sense in the relationship of parenthood. Mothers, and many fathers, would reject the notion that they take up the role of parent only in so far as it fits in with their life plans. Even looking at adult–adult relationships for many these are marked by love and care and not seen simply as a project for self-realisation (Jamieson 1999, p. 477).

3.2 Relational Life is Socially Good

The assumption behind the traditional autonomy approach is that family decisions are private and do not impact on society more broadly. People should therefore be left alone to make decisions about family life. That is mistaken. It overlooks the enormous social significance of families and their regulation.

A range of different reasons might be given for why family life is of broader social significance. For some stable relationships are central to thriving society. Lady Hale in Bull v Hall (2013) stated:

> The rights and obligations entailed in both marriage and civil partnership exist both to recognise and to encourage stable, committed, long-term relationships. It is very much in the public interest that intimate relationships be conducted in this way.

Bogenshneider (2013, p. 210) has set out five benefits she believes family life brings to society:

- Families as a foundation for generating productive workers
- Families as contributors to the rearing of caring, committed citizens
- Family policies and programmes as an efficient investment of public resources (e.g. to ensure child rearing and care for the elderly)
- Family policies and programmes as an efficient means of promoting positive child and youth development.

McClain (2006, Chap. 1) argues that families provide care and foster civil value. She sees much to do for law in ensuring marriage is an equal partnership and a fair sharing of care. The Government has a property role in fostering the conditions for families to operate and achieve these goals.

An assessment of the value of family life to the broader society would depend on the definition of the family used and would require a careful analysis of the disadvantages of family life. There is not space to fully debate the merits of the different advantages raised in the literature. In this book the central claim will be that it is in the context of family life that a substantial amount of care work is undertaken and that care work is of central value to social well-being.

The structures of family law significantly impact on how that care work is performed and who does it (Voena 2013, p. 2). As Martha Fineman has pointed out in her book *The Autonomy Myth* care for those who are unable to look after themselves is one of the most important jobs within society. She demonstrates how this care of dependents has been delegated to 'families' and thus been rendered unacknowledged in the public. Women in particular have, as a result, had their crucial societal contribution unrecognised and unrewarded. Fineman (2004, p. xviii) argues:

> [T]he family in [the traditional 'separate spheres' understanding of society] is positioned as a unique and private arena. I argue that this is an incorrect and unsustainable conception. The family is contained within the larger society, and its contours are defined as an institution by law. Far from being separate and private, the family interacts with and is

> acted upon by other societal institutions. I suggest the very relationship is not one of separation, but of symbiosis. It is very important to understand the roles assigned to the family in society—roles that otherwise might have to be played by other institutions, such as the market or the state.

The starting point of the response to care work must be that there are many individuals in society who need care. Assuming it is unacceptable for them to be left without care, it must be performed. The performance of that care comes at significant cost to those who provide it. Currently that largely falls on individuals within caring relationships. But if people stop caring, through choice or economic need, that burden would fall on the state (OECD 2013, 1). Carers (2010, p. 2) argues that the work of informal carers would cost £119 billion if the state had to perform it. By 2050, it is predicted the UK could be forced to spend 21.6 % of GDP on long-term care, pensions and health services to cope with the rise in elderly people requiring state assistance (OECD 2013). Carers (2012, p. 1) suggest that carers who give up work to care lose income of £1.3 billion annually.

There is, therefore, a clear economic case for the state being interested in how that care needs are met. If there is inadequate legal support or protection for those providing care and it falls on the state that will create serious economic consequences. Any decent society will also want to ensure that the distribution of the substantial care costs is fair (Himmelweit 2005, Chap. 1). Indeed a strong argument can be made that carers are undertaking a job on behalf of society that is a core obligation of a decent society (Herring 2013a, Chap. 4). Fineman (2000, p. 12) argues that there is a social duty to compensate carers as a result of their social contribution:

> If infants or ill persons are not cared for, nurtured, nourished, and perhaps loved, they will perish. We can say, therefore, that they owe an individual debt to their individual caretakers. But the obligation is not theirs alone—nor is their obligation confined only to their own caretakers. A sense of social justice demands a broader sense of obligation. Without aggregate caretaking, there could be no society, so we might say that it is caretaking labour that produces and reproduces society. Caretaking labour provides the citizens, the workers, the voters, the consumers, the students, and others who populate society and its institutions. The uncompensated labour of caretakers is an unrecognized subsidy, not only to individuals who directly receive it, but more significantly, to the entire society.

Martha Fineman suggests that it is best seen not as 'payment for care' but as a payment for debt. Busby (2011, p. 197) puts it this way:

> In the current context, legal intervention intended to provide an adequate response to the unpaid care/paid employment conflict can be manifested as a right, based on our shared humanity, to the equal distribution of resources on the basis of an individual's contribution in labour market terms and in respect of the unpaid provision of care.

Precisely the correct way to reward, acknowledge and protect care work is a complex matter (see Herring 2013a for a detail discussion). But there can be little doubt that our family lives; the regulation of those by the law; and the messages sent by that regulation can have a profound effect on care work and hence on wider society. Relationships of care and dependency need to be supported, nurtured and upheld, not hidden and downplayed (Verkerk 1999, p. 359). All of this means that we should not reduce family life to simply a private choice; an exercise of personal autonomy.

3.3 Obligations and Relational Autonomy

A further aspect of relational autonomy is that it emphasises the importance of relational obligations, as well as autonomy rights. These obligations cannot simply be subsumed within the traditional autonomy model by saying they have been voluntarily undertaken. The obligations attached to parenthood, for example, arise not from a specific choice of an individual, but from the relationship that exists (Leckey 2007, Chap. 1). It might be thought that the responsibilities and obligations that are emphasised by relational theorists are inconsistent with the value of autonomy. But the obligations of a relationship enable the relationship to work and flourish. They recognise the vulnerability that is created by intimate relationships and seeks to protect from being taken advantage of.

Typically in traditional liberal thought we start with a premise of freedom: we are free to act as we wish unless there is a particular obligation or duty that arises. The burden is on those who seek to claim there is a duty. A relational approach starts with responsibilities and connection as a norm. The question is not "is there a good reason to restrict my freedom", but rather "is it possible to have some freedom, given the responsibilities of those I am connected to" (Herring 2013a, Chap. 3). This might, to some seem shocking. Surely we should start with a presumption of freedom, rather than obligation. However, I suggest two reasons why we should not. First, that reflects the reality of life for most people. Our lives are not marked by freedom, but by our obligations to others. For most people it is obligations to children; friends or relations who are dependant on us; or wider social causes which mark our daily lives. Secondly, because that in it in our responsibilities that relationships flourish. As Curk (2011, p. 51) puts it: "We take responsibility for each other because we continue to need each other and because we establish meaningful relationships through taking responsibility for each other." Responsibilities therefore can be seen not as the corollary of rights, but rather rights are the tools we need to be able to carry our responsibilities. It is the performance of our relational responsibilities which should be key, not the maintenance of our freedoms (Williams 2002, p. 502).

An understanding of the nature of a commitment is important to the critique of traditional autonomy (Marin 2013, p. 6). Even where a commitment is undertaken by a choice, the obligations are outside the control of the agent. Indeed the whole point of a commitment is that it is "open ended" and you accept that the circumstances are unpredictable. In the words of the traditional marriage service partner take each other "for better, for worse; richer or poorer".

This is particularly significant in the care-giving context, where the demands of care are inherently unpredictable. As Marin (2013, p. 7) puts it:

> As their work of care is flexible (its demands of time and energy vary significantly over time, involve constant attentiveness to need and the ability to switch between different roles), responses have to be correspondingly flexible in order to be successful in undermining the processes that turn one's work of care into constraints to one's self-development; that is, they have to respond to the actual needs created by caregiving work, that is, to correspond to its variation over time, the demand of constant attentiveness, the demand of readiness to take on different roles, and so on. In other words, they have to take the form of open-ended responses. Caregivers are owed open-ended responses.

One consequence of this is that we cannot reduce caring obligations or compensation for losses caused by caring into some rigid formula, such as a contract. The other is that there is an inevitable tension between autonomy and the kind of commitment involved. Intimate relationships inevitably lead to a loss of freedom of choice as how to live your life on a daily basis. Carers frequently need to set aside their own preference and goals for the one they are caring for. At least they need to be ready to that at a moment's notice. That is a commitment they originally undertook, and is part of the caring relationship they chose to enter. Respecting their autonomous choice to enter such a relationship requires acknowledging the obligations and loss of autonomy that is associated with it.

3.4 Gender and Autonomy

Privileging individualist autonomy can operate in a way that disadvantages women (Friedman 2000, p. 24). It promotes the unattached unencumbered person as the norm. In advocating autonomy as the ideal, the obligation and responsibility of care work is downplayed. The assumption, indeed the ideal, is that everyone is responsible for their own well-being. We should be self-sufficient. Indeed being dependant on others or offering care to dependants it is seen as antagonistic to the autonomous ideal. As women undertake the majority of care work it disadvantages them. As Laufer-Ukeles (2008, p. 3) puts it:

> Revaluing nurture work does not mean that women must or should perform such work; rather, it is in the interest of society that such work be given proper accord. Gender makes a difference, and ignoring that difference creates unfairness. This unfairness must be addressed. An alternative to the gender neutral paradigm of divorce law must be identified. Gender difference in the context of divorce should be recognized by advocating support for the different and important contribution of caretaking. Such recognition will begin to address the hardships caretakers face at divorce.

In most, if not all, intimate relationships parties invest in varying ways and extents to the relationship. Putting central value on the autonomy of the parties to leave the relationship and pursue their own life goal will disadvantage the party who has invested more in it and has suffered economic or social disadvantage as a result. In most relationships, especially where there are children, that will be women. Gilligan (1982, p. 17) argues:

> Women's place in man's life-cycle has been that of nurturer, caretaker, and helpmate, the weaver of those networks of relationships on which she in turn relies. But while women have thus taken care of men, men have, in their theories of psychological development, as in their economic arrangements, tended to assume or devalue care. When the focus on individuation and individual achievement extends into adulthood and maturity is equated with personal autonomy, concern with relationships appears as a weakness of women rather than as a human strength.

The state clearly has an interest in promoting gender equality. It is clear the majority of care work is undertaken by women. In particular, the economic costs of care are largely borne by women. The state, therefore, has an interest in ensuring that the costs of care are fairly shared. As Himmelweit and Land (2008, p. 18) argue:

> The level of public expenditure on care is therefore a gender issue, since women have greater care needs than men and fewer resources to meet them. Inadequate funding also affects women in the paid care workforce and, when paid care is not forthcoming, as those more likely to end up providing unpaid care. Thus, inadequate spending on care is effectively a transfer of resources (unpaid labour) from women to relieve taxpayers, disproportionately men, of their responsibilities to provide for the most vulnerable citizens.

It is not just in economic terms that the issue is important for women. Williams (2010, p. 4) argues that the treatment of care as 'domestic' has significant impact for women's live more broadly:

> That gender system, inherited from the nineteenth century, divides daily life neatly into the mutually exclusive realms of public life and domestic life. Separate spheres imputes specific, and different, biological and psychological characteristics to men and women. Women are deemed too good for the nasty and brutish world of commerce in which men—so the story goes—thrive. From this story stems a set of interlocking assumptions: that it is natural for women to take sole responsibility for child care, that doing so fulfils women's deepest nature and so makes them happy, that men are competitive and ambitious and thus naturally suited to employment but not to caregiving, and that homemakers' economic vulnerability in breadwinner-homemaker households is no big deal.

The attitude towards care therefore reflects and reinforces what society regards as of value and worth. In so far as these downplay the significance of what women do, it works against their interests.

More needs to be said about the nature of the gender gap. There are three aspects to it. First, there is a gap in the performance of care work. Women perform significantly more care work then men. Second, women's place in the workplace is markedly lower than men. Women are paid on average 14.9 % lower than men; are far more likely to undertake part time and other low paid jobs. Third, women are significantly more likely to need care than men. Glendinning et al. (2009, p. 3) explain:

> Caring is gender-based; women take the brunt of caring and are also the majority of care receivers. This gender bias is even more marked when physically intimate and/or emotionally more demanding tasks are involved. The proportion of men caring is smaller; they care for fewer hours per week; and the tasks they undertake are less onerous and stressful. Broadly speaking, the pattern is very similar to that found in relation to housework and

childcare; women are more likely to organise paid work around care, while men tend to organise care around work.

Gornick and Meyers (2003, p. 21) argue for a range of solutions to deal with the problems:

> The role for public policy would be to encourage the dissolution of gender divisions in the home through the use of parental leave; to transform the workplace from its current androcentrism to reduce working hours and become more flexible to allow for better work/care balance; and to protect parents' rights for time to care and children's rights for quality care through provision of high-quality childcare provided by well-trained and well-paid care workers.

Seeing caring as a central aspect of citizenship and an essential part of a democracy is very helpful. Sevenhuihsen (2000, p. 6) goes on to explain how this radically changes the approach the state take to responsibilities:

> An ethics of care implies a radically different argument on the relationship between morality and politics, and thus about responsibility and obligation. Because it starts from a relational ontology, it focuses primarily on the question of what politics could mean for the safeguarding of responsibility and relationship in human interactions. A relational approach would start from the idea that policy-making needs elaborated insights into the way individuals frame their responsibilities in the context of actual social practices and how they handle the moral dilemmas that go with the conflicting responsibilities of care for self, others, and the relationship between them.

The fact, however, that care is valuable to the state does not mean that the state necessarily needs to support it. There are plenty of activities that the state does not support, despite their social value. Himmelweit (2005, p. 32) gives some powerful reasons why the state should not simply leave care alone:

> Without intervention people may be less willing and able to fulfil caring norms, which may thereby be eroded. Those who assume caring responsibilities despite such pressures will pay a higher price for doing so and may have less influence on policy than those conforming more to increasingly less caring dominant norms. Not to adopt a generous strategy for caring now will shift power away from those who continue to care, erode caring norms, and make it more difficult to adopt a more caring strategy in the future. Without such a strategy, standards and availability of care will fall with high cost to society as a whole and fall particularly heavily on those who continue to care.

One of the great benefits of this approach is that it moves away from the idea that care work is some kind of option extra that especially good people undertake. Rather it sees care as a central aspect of citizenship. It is not performing care work that is seen as surprising. If care work is a taken for granted responsibility for citizens then all aspects of society need to be reworked around that responsibility to ensure it can be done.

Sometimes the concept of equality is used to argue against any gender argument. We should treat men and women equally, it is suggested. Both have choices to make and if a woman decides to, for example, undertake child care rather than seek employment she should not comply. However, as Diduck and Kaganas (2013, p. 279) argue that a difference in treatment can be justified "to compensate for differences and disadvantage created by institutions such as marriage or structural conditions such as lack of public support for child care. In this light, different treatment might be necessary to ensure that disadvantage is not suffered by one group disproportionately to another". In any event there is no argument here for treatment men and women differently. The argument is that those who undertake care work, be they men or women need to have their interests protects.

3.5 Distinguishing Relational and Traditional Autonomy

At this point it should be emphasised that most supporters of the traditional liberal view of autonomy reject such a description of autonomy. Some people may choose to live their life in an unattached way; others, fortunately, choose to live a relational life. The criticisms made of liberal autonomy, it is said, are better directed at the choices people make, rather than the concept of autonomy itself. This objection has some validity. It is true that some relational autonomy writing has used a "straw man" version of autonomy. However, relational autonomy is a distinct approach. Four points should be emphasised.

First, autonomy must be seen in the context of the broader social and legal picture. Becker (1999, p. 22) writes: 'patriarchy values power, control, autonomy, independence, toughness, invulnerability, strength, aggressiveness, rationality, detachment (being non-emotional), and other traditionally masculine attributes that have proven effective in the battle against other men.' Once put in the context of other values that society and law values autonomy can be said to play its part in promoting individualism. Individualism ignores the complex web of relations and connections which make up most people's lives. The reality for everyone, but in our society particularly women, is that it is the values of inter-dependence and connection, rather than self-sufficiently and independence, which reflect their reality. People do not understand their family lives as involving clashes of individual rights or interests, but rather as a working through of relationships. The muddled give and take of everyday family life where sacrifices are made and benefits gained, without them being totted up on some giant familial star chart, chimes more with everyday family life than the image of independent interests and rights.

Eekelaar (2013) questions whether it is right to tie in individualism with selfishness. While he accepts that increased individualism has meant that institutions (such as marriage) and communities (such as formal religious groups) have waned in power, that does not mean individuals are not feeling communal ties. He questions Singer (1995, p. 2)'s claim of the dominant twin assumptions of American society as being "looking out for number one" and "getting more money." He notes that the rise of "individualism" has also been marked by "new duties" including avoiding discrimination on the grounds of gender, race, disability, sexual orientation; a duty to safeguard the health and safety of others, and especially vulnerable people; and an awareness of the importance of respecting other people's human rights.

Applying Eekelaar's analysis to family life one might argue that even if the ties of marriage are weakened by more ready divorce or cohabitation, there are still powerful moral changes with reduced acceptance of domestic abuse and, in theory at least, a commitment to egalitarian roles within marriage. More broadly, as Eekelaar mentions, even if there is a weakening of an obligation to broader family members by virtue of the blood tie alone, a close interaction with the family member and family will increase that obligation. Indeed Douglas et al. (2011, p. 245) claims that in relation to testamentary disposition, family bonds remain strong.

This analysis is convincing. The argument promoted here is not that people are being more self-centred, rather than the language and tools of individual autonomy incorrectly represent people as isolated individuals and so fail to resonate with the lived-in experience of people's lives and adequately promote relationships or protect people within them. Individual concepts of autonomy make legal arguments work well for those perusing individualistic autonomy projects. The language used and the legal structure promote individualised ways. The widespread lack of care work in the legal system (Herring 2013a) demonstrates the way autonomy, even if on its surface neutral, preferences an individualised conception of it.

Second, relational autonomy is highly sensitive to the way in which our relationships constitute identity and are integral to autonomy. So it is not, as traditional autonomy, (even a version sensitive to relational concerns) would have it, that we form our goals for our life and then seek to use our relationships to peruse those goals. Our goals are formed by and within the context of our relationship and in a context in which talk of using a relationship to achieve one's goals makes no sense because identities become fused. This means that an attempt to ascertain whether someone has capacity and what their autonomous wish is can only properly made if assessed within the context of their relationships. A capacity test should therefore consider whether an individual, with the support of the family and friends, is able to made a decision.

Relational autonomy does not reject the notion of the self. As Nedelsky (2012, pp. 3–5) explains the self is *constituted* by interactive relationships with others. This means that "selves become who they are—their identities, their capacities, their desires—through the relationships in which they participate." Of course supporters of traditional liberal understandings of autonomy will readily accept that relationships are valuable and important to our selves. However, relational autonomy makes a bolder claim, that these relationships constitute the self. That means that autonomous decisions can only be understood in the context of those relationships. So, we do not start from the atomised self and ask what choices they have made and whether this includes entering relationships. Rather the relationships are not means of perusing an individual's autonomy, but define the individual. Reece (2003, p. 121) uses the example of readily available divorce:

> Ready divorce does not promote authenticity because uncommitted relationships do not allow us to explore our whole selves but only to experience pleasure. On this view, the state respect our self-determination not by enabling us to stand back from our relationships and commitments but by encouraging a deeper immersion in and understanding of them.

She is not, here, making the case for a rigid divorce law, however she acknowledges that part of respecting autonomy may involve acknowledging that choices involving a degree of commitment and the undertaking of obligations are, in fact, important for a rich and flourishing life. In recognising the obligations of relationships the law is in one sense restricting autonomy, but on the other hand is respecting autonomy by providing a framework so that people can enter into committed relationships.

Robert Leckey (2007, Chap. 7) has correctly identified two strands of thinking among those writing from a relational perspective. One strand seeks to be content neutral, respecting all relationships that people may choose to enter. The other has a stronger vision about what kinds of relationships the law should seek to uphold. In this book the latter, stronger, approach is preferred for two reasons. First, we need to mark out those oppressive relationships which undermine autonomy by depriving a party of the opportunity to form their own aspirations and visions for their life. These, in the family context, are typically marked by domestic abuse. Second, it is "thick" relationships, to use Leckey's terminology, marked by care and deep interdependence which are most in need of the support and protection of the law

A third distinction, is a relational autonomy perspective is more aware than traditional autonomy of the way relationships can impair autonomy. It realises that "our decisions" are in fact decisions reached within a relational context and so not straight forwardly ours. It is, therefore, peculiarly alert to the difficulties in determining the extent to which someone's decision may be result of manipulation at the hands of others. Oshana (2006, p. 72) argues 'autonomy calls for a measure of substantive independence from other persons and from social roles and traditions of a variety deemed to be inhospitable to autonomy' Relational autonomy supporters will accept that some relationships are destructive of an individual's autonomy. The challenge is then to define how we determine which relationships a model of autonomy should promote and which it should regard as destructive of autonomy. Nedelsky (2012, p. 122) argues, '[p]art of the reason relational autonomy is so important is that it is part of what enables people to extricate themselves from bad relationships as well as to transform the structures that shaped those relationships'. The concern in particular is that a person in an oppressed relationship or member of an oppressive group will internalizes the values of the group reducing their own self work and trust. There is, as already argued, a sense in which that is an inevitable part of humanity. However, there comes a point where the pressures of the group negate any sense of choice by the individual.

Sherwin and Winsby (2011, p. 182) write:

> For agents to be autonomous, they must be able to resist the options that help to sustain their own oppression. To ensure that conditions are such that the exercise of a reasonably high degree of autonomy is possible, it is sometimes necessary to try to correct limitations inherent in the background conditions of each person's social location.

The question, therefore, seems to be whether the relational and social context is such that a person is self-governing, as Mackenzie (2008, p. 512) put it. She explains that this means that an agent "regards herself as the legitimate source of the authority, as able, and authorized, to speak for herself," and that "such attitudes towards oneself can only be sustained in relations of intersubjective recognition".

As Stoljar (2011, p. 376) puts it:

> A person who is suffering a harm of oppression such as false consciousness or deformed desire is not autonomous with respect to the relevant ideology or desire. This agent may value that which is oppressive to her in a weak sense—in the sense of being drawn to, preferring, or even endorsing, that which is oppressive to her. But she is not autonomous until she has subjected her desire to evaluation in a strong sense and to discriminate whether it is "right or wrong, better or worse, higher or lower".

Feminists have been particularly astute to the way that women can be defined by male-dominated society and take on the expectations and views expected of them (Nedelsky 2012, p. 54).

There is an inevitable tension here for supporters of relational autonomy. The more our relational nature is emphasised, the harder it is define where the boundary between being oppressed within a relationship to such an extent that one loses autonomy and where one is simply deeply embedded in relationship. Nedelsky (2012, p. 118) is adamant we must hold on to autonomy and provides a way through the dilemma:

> The central problem in the modern administrative state is no longer the traditional liberal objective of protecting individual autonomy by keeping the state at bay. The problem is how to protect and enhance the autonomy of those who are *within* the (many) spheres of state power.

Fourth, as we have seen there can be tension between the notion of respecting the autonomy to enter a committed relationship and the freedom to act as you wish when that commitment is under strain. It is here that relational autonomy, to a greater extent than traditional autonomy, may be willing to put restrictions on the current autonomy to respect the deeper relational autonomy the person wishes. Family lawyers should see no surprise in this. We expect parents to pay child support, even though that is against their interests. We give effect to parental responsibilities even if against the current wishes of the parent. Inter-spouse obligations are enforced in divorce. These can all be justified as such obligations create an option a person can enter. If we think it helpful or good for people to be able to enter committed relationships then the law needs to enforce those commitments and obligations. They cannot readily be dispensed with in the name of autonomy.

Before leaving this issue, it must be accepted that there is much debate over those attracted to a relational approach should support or oppose rights; or advocate an alternative approach based on an ethic of care. I do not want to enter that debate here (see Herring 2013a, b). I will assume for now that if only because the current legal and political climate is rights-soaked, the politically most astute course of action is to retain the language of rights (Mendus 1995, p. 10), including the language of autonomy. The writing on relational autonomy provides an approach which is in tune with the dominant discourse in legal writing.

References

Baker K (2011) Family, the law, and the constitution(s). Available at SSRN: http://ssrn.com/abstract=1106423
Barclay L (2000) Autonomy and the social self. In: Mackenzie C, Stoljar N (eds) Relational Autonomy. Oxford University Press, New York, pp 52–71
Barvosa-Carter E (2007) Mestiza autonomy as relational autonomy: Ambivalence and the social character of free will. J Polit Philos 15:1–21
Becker M (1999) Patriarchy and inequality: towards a substantive feminism. University of Chicago Legal Forum 21–52
Bogenschneider K (2013) Making a global case for family policy. In: Abela A, Walker J (eds) Contemporary issues in family studies. Wiley Blackwell, Oxford
Busby N (2011) A right to care? Oxford University Press, Oxford
Carers UK (2010) Valuing carers. Carers UK, London
Carers UK (2012) Growing the care market. Carers UK, London
Carle S (2005) Theorizing agency. Am Univ Law Rev 55:307–365
Code L (1991) Second persons. In: Code L (ed) What can she known? Feminist theory and the construction of knowledge. Cornell University Press, Ithica
Curk P (2011) Passions, dependencies, selves. In: Lind C, Keating H, Bridgeman J (eds) Taking responsibility, law and the changing family. Ashgate, Aldershot, pp 51–67
Diduck A, Kaganas F (2013) Family law, gender and the state. Hart Publishing, Oxford
Donchin A (2000) Autonomy, interdependence, and assisted suicide: respecting boundaries/crossing lines. Bioethics 14:187–212
Douglas G, Woodward H, Humphrey A (2011) Enduring love? Attitudes to family and inheritance law in England and Wales. J Law Soc 38:245–275
Eekelaar J (2013) Self-restraint: Social Norms, individualism and the family. Theor Inquiries Law 13:75–96
Fineman M (2000) Cracking the foundational myths: independence, autonomy and self-sufficiency. Am Univ J Gend Soc Policy Law 8:13–29
Fineman M (2004) The autonomy myth. New Press, New York
Friedman M (2000) Autonomy, social disruption, and women. In: MacKenzie C, Stoljar N (eds) Relational autonomy. Oxford University Press, Oxford
Gergen KJ (2009) Relational being: beyond self and community. Oxford University Press, New York
Gergen KJ (2011) Relational being: a brief introduction. J Constructivist Psychol 24:280–282
Gilligan C (1982) In a different voice. Harvard University Press, Cambridge
Glendinning C, Tjadens F, Arksey H, Morée M, Moran N, Nies H (2009) Care provision within families and its socio-economic impact on care providers. University of York, York
Glendon MA (1989) The transformation of family law. University of Chicago Press, Chicago
Gornick J, Meyers M (2003) Families that work: policies for reconciling parenthood and employment. Russell Sage Foundation, New York
Herring J (2009) Relational autonomy and rape. In: Day Sclater S, Ebtehaj F, Jackson E, Richards M (eds) Regulating autonomy: sex, reproduction and family. Hart Publishing, Oxford
Herring J (2013a) Caring and the law. Hart Publishing, Oxford
Herring J (2013b) Forging a relational approach: best interests or human rights? Med Law Int 13:32–54
Himmelweit S (2005) Can we afford (not) to care: prospects and policy. Open University, Buckingham
Himmelweit S, Land H (2008) Reducing gender inequalities to create a sustainable care. Joseph Rowntree Foundation, York
Jamieson L (1999) Intimacy transformed? A critical look at the 'pure relationship'. Sociology 33:477–496
Johnson A (1997) Gender Knot. Temple University Press, Philadelphia

Laufer-Ukeles P (2008) Selective recognition of gender difference in the law: Revaluing the caretaker role. Harvard J Law Gend 31:1–36

Leckey R (2007) Contracting claims and family law feuds. Univ Toronto Law J 57:1–41

Mackenzie C, Stoljar N (eds) (2000) Relational autonomy. Oxford University Press, New York

Mackenzie C (2008) Relational autonomy, normative authority and perfectionism. J Soc Philos 39:512–533

Marin M (2013) Care, oppression and marriage. Hypatia forthcoming

McClain L (2006) The place of families: fostering capacity, equality and responsibility. Harvard University Press, Cambridge

Mendus S (1995) Human rights in political theory. Polit Stud 43:10–32

Mulinari D, Sandell K (2009) A feminist re-reading of theories of late modernity: Beck, Giddens and the location of gender. Crit Sociol 35:493–512

Nedelsky J (1989) Reconceiving autonomy: sources, thoughts and possibilities. Yale J Law Feminism 1:7–36

Nedelsky J (2012) Law's relations. Oxford University Press, Oxford

OECD (2013), Huge elderly care bill threatens family ties. The Telegraph (available at www.telegraph.co.uk/news/politics/8501333/OECD-huge-elderly-care-bill-threatens-family-ties.html)

Oshana M (2006) Personal autonomy in society. Ashgate, Aldershot

Reece H (2003) Divorcing responsibly. Hart Publishing, Oxford

Ribbens McCarthy J (2012) The powerful relational language of 'family'. The Sociological Review 1:75–94

Sanders L (2013) "You're not you": caregiver autonomy and disability rights. Available at http://wpsa.research.pdx.edu/meet/2012/sanders_yny.pdf

Sevenhuijsen S (2000) Caring in the third way: the relation between obligation, responsibility and acre in third way discourse. Crit Soc Policy 20:5–24

Shaw S (2008) Family leisure and changing ideologies of parenthood. Sociol Compass 2:1–16

Sherwin S, Winsby M (2011) A relational perspective on autonomy for older adults residing in nursing homes. Health Expectations 14:182–190

Singer P (1995) How are we to live? Ethics in an age of self-interest. Prometheus Books, London

Slife B, Richardson F (2011) Is Gergen's relational being relational enough? J Constructivist Psychol 24:304–313

Smart C (2007) Personal life. Polity Press, Cambridge

Stoljar N (2011) Informed consent and relational conceptions of autonomy. J Med Philos 36:375–384

Verkerk M (1999) A care perspective on coercion and autonomy. Bioethics 13:358–379

Verkerk M (2001) The care perspective and autonomy. Med Health Care Philos 4:289–294

Voena A (2013) Yours, mine and ours: do divorce laws affect the intertemporal behavior of married couples. Available at SSRN: http://ssrn.com/abstract=2007575

Williams F (2002) The presence of feminism in the future of welfare. Econ Soc 31:502–519

Williams J (2010) Reshaping the work-family debate: why men and class matter. Harvard University Press, Cambridge MA

Cases

Bull v Hall [2013] UKSC 36

National Coalition for Gay and Lesbian Equality v Minister of Justice, 1999 (1) SA 6

Chapter 4
Applying Relational Autonomy to Family Law

So far we have seen that relationships are key to individual's identity and to the good of society. However, relationships, especially involving care, can cause serious loss and leave a party vulnerable. We need therefore to respond to people's autonomy rights in a relational way. What is the significance of this for family law?

4.1 A Family Law Which Fosters Relationships

Relational autonomy will seek an active role for the state in forging policies that bolster and support relationships. Traditionally this has been through marriage (West 1998, p. 706), but it might done be through other statuses based on relationships or through support for relationships of care (Herring 2014; Bartlett 1998). The state is required to create the conditions where a person can exercise their autonomy by entering a relationship which receives support and protection by society; and ensures a person is not disadvantaged by entering such a relationship. As Nedelsky (1993, p. 343) argues, the state must attend to:

> conditions that foster people's capacity to form caring, responsible and intimate relationships with each other—as family members, friends, members of a community, and citizens of a state.

Brinig and Nock (2000, p. 11) argue that the availability of state supported forms of relationship provide a benefits for society and the individuals:

> The normative expectation of permanence and unconditional love is the basis for collective trust that the relationship in question will function in its prescribed way. For couples, that means that others will trust that they will pursue intimacy in socially recognized (i.e., normative) ways. For parents, that means trusting that they will provide an environment within which children can flourish. In return for conforming to community norms, that is, people in relationships are given various legal and other supports that further encourage and promote the relationship.

J. Herring, *Relational Autonomy and Family Law*, SpringerBriefs in Law,
DOI: 10.1007/978-3-319-04987-8_4, © The Author(s) 2014

Such arguments raise a host of issues. While public support and recognition of a relationship is important, whether that needs to be in the form of a legal status, or even in the form of state-approved status may be questioned. Indeed for some families, no doubt, the support and approval of their friends, community or faith is of far greater significant than any legal or state recognition (Eekelaar and Maclean 2005). Nevertheless the state has a role in fostering the circumstances in which dependent relationships receive recognition and support. While marriage as it is presently understood is far too narrow (and too broad) for that role (Herring 2013; Frelich Appleton 2013), Minow and Lyndon Shanley (1996, p. 4) make a powerful point:

> while loving and committed relationships might presumably exist without the state, there are in fact no family or family-like relationships that are not shaped by social practices and state action.

Marriage as it currently stands seems unfit for the job (Herring 2014). Chambers (2013, p. 124) summarises the primary criticisms of it:

> Practical, empirical harms to women resulting from marriage include the contingent facts that marriages tend to reinforce the gendered division of labour, which itself means that women earn less and are less independent than men; that they reinforce the idea that women do most of the housework, even if they work outside the home, which saps their energies and dignity; and that domestic violence may be exacerbated by marital concepts of entitlement and ownership.

One might also add its role in reinforcing heterosexual relations as the norm. Whatever the justifications of such claims, and clearly they are controversial, it does not seem impossible that marriage could be reformulated in a more egalitarian way and the law could ensure mitigation is made of these disadvantages. Perhaps more to the point it is not clear that a complete absence of legal or state input into the structures or support of intimate relationships (e.g. by leaving relationships as a matter of contract or utterly outside formal regulation) would not also demonstrate the undesirable characteristic that Chambers mentions. Indeed, assuming the nature of intimate relationships remained unchanged, we would lose the power of the law to remedy those disadvantages at the end of the relationships through court orders. Leaving relationships unregulated would cause significant harms. We need therefore a form of fostering of relationships marked by care, to peruse the good of society; the protection of those in the relationship and an enhancement of their autonomy.

4.2 A Family Law Which Acknowledges the Significance of Relationships

Under the traditional liberal approach, the freedom of autonomy of an individual in the family context must be weighed against the claims of their partner or children or perhaps some state interests (Eichner 2007). In the European Court of Human

Rights family cases are typically seen as requiring a balance between the competing rights of the family members (Choudhry and Herring 2010, Chap. 2). This, however, is predicated on the basis that we *can* separate out the interests of a parent and a child. But, one cannot separate out the interests of a parent and a child or the interests of intimate partners. They are intertwined (Herring 1999). To harm a child is to harm the person caring for the child; and to harm the carer is to harm the child. We shall be exploring later the practical significance of this point.

4.3 A Family Law that Protects Those in Relationships from Abuse

Entering an intimate relationship carries with it risks. As will be explored below an intimate relationship can create a risk of violence and abuse. There is certainly a danger with relational autonomy, with its emphasis on promoting relationships, being represented as failing to appreciate the possibility of abuse within relationship.

Feder Kittay (2007, p. 468), writing from an ethic of care perspective, is aware of the dangers of promoting every relationship marked by care. She argues:

> Total self-sacrifice, the annihilation of the self in favor of the cared for, is neither demanded by the practice of care nor is it justifiable, for one can see that a relationship requires two selves, not one self in which the other is subsumed and consumed. A care ethic is not a mere reaction to individualism, but it tempers individualism by insisting that the relationships in which we stand help to constitute the individual we have become, are now and will be in the future.

The tensions between promoting care and protection are highlighted in the care ethicist literature by the distinction between an ethic of care and an ethic of justice. Gilligan (1982) first distinguished an ethic of care from an ethic of justice. Held (2006, p. 15) explains the difference:

> An ethic of justice focuses on questions of fairness, equality, individual rights, abstract principles, and the consistent application of them. An ethic of care focuses on attentiveness, trust, responsiveness to need, narrative nuance, and cultivating caring relations. Whereas an ethic of justice seeks a fair solution between competing individual interests and rights, an ethic of care sees the interest of carers and cared-for as importantly intertwined rather than as simply competing.

However, Held (2006, p. 17), arguably the world's leading contemporary care ethicist, argues that an ethic of care includes justice:

> There can be care without justice. There has historically been little justice in the family, but care and life have gone on without it. There can be no justice without care, however, for without care no child would survive and there would be no persons to respect.

Held is correct to emphasize that justice must be included with an effective, ethic of care, although its role should be to support caring relationships. The same is true of a broader approach based on relational autonomy. A relational approach offers insights into the wrong at the heart of domestic abuse and provides a powerful argument for intervention.

4.4 A Family Law Which Remedies Financial Disadvantages that Result from Relationship

Relationships create risks of financial disadvantage. It is essential that the law protects individuals from these dangers. First, as a basic matter of fairness. Second, to ensure the fear of serious disadvantage does not put people off entering these socially useful relationships. Third, because the disadvantage that can be caused by an remedied loss cause wider social impacts (e.g. gender disadvantage).

An approach based on relational autonomy would, therefore, have some scepticism about the move to unregulated mediation. To be clear, it would not oppose negotiation by parties advised by lawyers, seeking to find an agreement within the parameters of what a court is likely to order. However, it would reject an argument that family disputes should simply be resolved by the parties themselves. There are several reasons. First, an understanding of the power of relationships between the parties means that we need to acknowledge the vulnerabilities of the parties to manipulation and exploitation within the mediation process. On the breakdown of the relationship leaving a couple to mediation as Eekelaar (2013a, p. 417) puts it "could look like abandoning them to the law of the jungle."

In a helpful study Wilson (2011) explores the potential impact of the law not regulating the breakdown marriage or intimate relationships. He focusses on religion. As he suggests if the law failed to regulate disputes at the end of a relationship and left this entirely to people's personal choices, religion would undoubted play a role in the choices made. As his survey show under religious regimes women would do badly in terms of responses of domestic abuse; child custody and financial orders.

Second, there must be a rejection of the argument in the argument in the Family Justice review that disputes between family members arose from their "own personal choices". As Eekelaar (2011, p. 316) argues, that is a bizarre argument. Most legal disputes result from a personal choice: be that to be employed or enter a contract or apply for asylum. It does not make sense to suggest that as a legal dispute comes about as a result of a choice it does not deserve legal aid, especially where the choice made is a reasonable one. As Eekelaar suggests a better case may be that these disputes involves deeply personal matters and that it is best for the law to stay out of the "intimate sphere". However, that argument seems at its strongest when the relationship is intact and is a strong one. Where the couple are in dispute, the protection of the intimate space is no longer required.

Third, leaving the resolution of disputes at the end of family life to the couple themselves ignores the important social consequences of these decisions. The current law fails adequately to respond to the financial inequalities caused in a relationship. As Fineman (2004, p. 228) has said,

> [I]n our political ideology, dependency is considered to be a private matter. It is the family, not the state or the market, that assumes responsibility for both the inevitable dependent—the child or other biologically or developmentally dependent person—and the derivative dependent—the caretaker. The institution of the family operates structurally and ideologically to free markets from considering or accommodating dependency. The state is cast as a default institution, providing minimal, grudging and stigmatized assistance should families fail.

If we are to move to a system of family law which ensure that family life does not work in this way, then it is essential that the law provides adequate and effective compensation for disadvantages caused by caring obligations within intimate relationships. As Hale (2011, p. 10) asks:

> Do we want to encourage responsible families, [and, I would add, societies] in which people are able to compromise their place in the world outside the home for the sake of their partners, their children and their elderly or disabled relatives [and again I would add society], and can be properly compensated for this if things go wrong? I continue to hope that we do. But I wonder whether we really believe in equality in marriage.

In an excellent analysis Diduck (2011, p. 314) has summarised the key role for family law in this way:

> Family law determines the responsibilities of individuals to each other and by extension, the responsibilities of families and the state and the community to each other. Whether it is about money, care of children, employment, income support, or housing, the purpose of family law is to allocate and enforce responsibility for those responsibilities. This analysis reveals that when judges determine responsibility for financial and care responsibilities post-divorce they do so through a plurality of discourses which jostle for dominance from time to time.

As this quote acknowledges family law plays an important social role. Intimate relationships, especially relationships of care are an inevitable and fundamental part of the human condition. But undertaking care involves costs. This is important work. As Eichner (2011, p. 306) puts it:

> Because of this, and the critical role that sound families play in the lives of thriving citizens and a flourishing society, a government committed to human dignity must do more when it comes to families than simply seek to adopt a position of neutrality. It must, instead, actively seek to construct a network of policies that support families and the caretaking and human development functions that they fulfil.

This model is described by Eichner (2011, p. 305) as the "supportive state". She argues:

> families appropriately bear responsibility for the day-today caring for (or arranging the care for) children and for meeting other dependency needs. Meanwhile, the state bears the responsibility for structuring societal institutions in ways that help families meet their caretaking needs and promote adequate human development. In this way, the supportive

> state seeks to balance the important goods of caretaking and human development with other important goods that its policies can implicate, including individual autonomy and sex equality.

This raises a host of important issues, which go beyond the scope of this book (see Case 2001). Precisely the relationships between parents and state over the financial costs of child care is subject to much debate (Ferguson 2008). For now, it is suffice to say the state has a very legitimate interest, indeed a crucial interest, in providing a framework for meeting care needs. If individuals are left free to negotiate for themselves how these are to be balanced this is will undermine the value of care.

4.5 The Role of Law in Intact Families

While relational autonomy would support the bolstering of relationships and the promotion of fairness within them, this is not, of course, restricted to the law. Eekelaar (2013b) has helpful distinguished between three models of how the law can relate to the family. He is generally somewhat suspicious of legal intervention in family life. He refers to the bureaucracy of the law which has "little sensitivity to the nuances of the contexts of many personal relationships". Intimate relationships need space and privacy to develop trust. However, he is also wary of using the law to reinforce relational obligations with coercion because families and communities have history of oppressing disadvantaged members. On the other hand he acknowledges that "law is the only safeguard individuals have *against the* exercise of power." He explore three models. The "authorisation model" is one where the state "*allow[s] families* to define the obligations their members owe to one another, and recognize their authority as having the force of law." This he sees as having the dangers of allowing the oppression of individual members. The "delegation model" he defines as where "the *state* prescribes what those norms should be, and expects families to follow them as delegates of the state's authority". The model, the one favoured by Eekelaar is the "purposive abstention" model, "where the state refrains from legally prescribing the content of norms within families, although it may seek to influence them in other ways, while the general law remains operative in the background."

This book will now explore the practical application of these issues to some specific questions.

References

Bartlett K (1998) Saving the family from the reformers. U C Davis L Rev 31:809–854
Brinig M, Nock S (2000) Covenant and contract. Regent U Law Rev 12:9–26
Chambers C (2013) The marriage-free state. Proc Aristot Soc 113:123–143

Choudhry S, Herring J (2010) European human rights and family law. Hart Publishing, Oxford
Diduck A (2011) What is Family Law for? Curr Legal Probl 64:287–314
Eekelaar J (2011) Not of the highest importance: family justice under threat. J Soc Welf Family Law 33:311–317
Eekelaar J (2013a) Then and now—family law's direction of travel. J Soc Welf Family Law 35:415–426
Eekelaar J (2013b) Self-restraint: social norms, individualism and the family. Theor Inq Law 13:75–96
Eekelaar J, Maclean M (2005) The significance of marriage: contrasts between white British and ethnic minority groups in England. Law Policy 27:379–399
Eichner M (2007) Principles of the law of relationships among adults. Family Law Q 41:433–454
Eichner M (2011) Beyond private ordering. J Am Acad Matrim Lawyers 23:305–346
Feder Kittay E (2007) Searching for an overlapping consensus: a secular care ethics feminist responds to religious feminists. Univ St Thomas Law J 4:468–488
Ferguson L (2008) Family, social inequalities, and the persuasive force of interpersonal obligation. Int J Law Policy Family 22:61–92
Fineman M (2004) The autonomy myth. New Press, New York
Frelich Appleton S (2013) Family law's equality project in our empirical age. In: McClain L, Cere D (eds) What is parenthood?. New York University Press, New York
Gilligan C (1982) In a different voice. Harvard University Press, Cambridge
Hale B (2011) Equality and autonomy in family law. J Soc Welf Family Law 33:3–14
Held V (2006) The ethics of care. Oxford University Press, Oxford
Herring J (1999) The welfare principle and the rights of parents. In: Bainham A, Lindley B, Richards M (eds) What is a parent?. Hart Publishing, Oxford
Herring J (2013) Caring and the law. Hart Publishing, Oxford
Herring J (2014) Making family law more careful. In: Wallbank J, Herring J (2013) Vulnerabilities, care and family law. Routledge, Abingdon, pp. 43–59
Minow M, Lyndon Shanley M (1996) Relational rights: revisioning the family in liberal political theory and law. Hypatia 11:4
Nedelsky J (1993) Property in potential life? A relational approach to choosing legal categories. Can J Law Jurisprud 6:343
West R (1998) Universalism, liberal theory, and the problem of gay marriage. Fla State Univ Law Rev 25:705–730
Wilson R (2011) The perils of privatized marriage. In: Nichols J (ed) Marriage and divorce in a multi-cultural context: reconsidering the boundaries of civil law and religion. Cambridge University Press, Cambridge

Chapter 5
Examples of Application

5.1 Pre-marriage Contracts

Traditionally in English law pre-marriage contracts have not been enforceable (Morley 2006). However, a sharp turn in approach occurred following the decision of the Supreme Court in *Radmacher v Granatino* (2010), with the majority concluding

> [t]he court should give effect to a nuptial agreement that is freely entered into by each party with a full appreciation of its implications unless in the circumstances prevailing it would not be fair to hold the parties to their agreement. (para 75)

Notably at the heart of their reasoning was the importance of autonomy:

> The reason why the court should give weight to a nuptial agreement is that there should be respect for individual autonomy. The court should accord respect to the decision of a married couple as to the manner in which their financial affairs should be regulated. It would be paternalistic and patronising to override their agreement simply on the basis that the court knows best. This is particularly true where the parties' agreement addresses existing circumstances and not merely the contingencies of an uncertain future. (para 78)

This kind of autonomy argument has been the basis of the case for allowing enforcement of pre-nuptial agreements. Cretney (2003, p. 403), one of England's finest family lawyers, has argued that the law should 'allow husband and wife the liberty…to decide for themselves the terms of their own partnership.' Even some feminists have joined in support for such contracts as a way of giving the parties the freedom the depart from outdated patriarchal models of marriage (Deech 1977). Singer (1992, p. 1443) argues:

> [H]onoring the decisional autonomy of those individuals and groups who have traditionally been disfavored by the law promises both to enhance personal freedom and promote equality goals. Substituting private for public control over the formation and structure of the family relationship seems to offer a similar double benefit: it expands the opportunities for the exercise of personal choice while affirming the inherent equality of the sexes.

J. Herring, *Relational Autonomy and Family Law*, SpringerBriefs in Law,
DOI: 10.1007/978-3-319-04987-8_5,

Significantly Martha Fineman has been supportive of using contracts to determine the responsibilities between adults (Fineman 2004, pp. 133–134). She believes this would advance individual freedom and gender equality and remove unjustified distinctions between married and unmarried couples. It would also open up the notion of family life to a broader range of forms of relationships, than that which the heterosexual model of marriage permits (Kachroo 2007). These arguments will be rejected in this book. A strong argument against enforcement of pre-nuptial agreements can be made from the perspective of relational autonomy.

First, there is the argument that only very rarely can there be an equality of bargaining power between parties contemplating marriage. Feminists have expressed concerns that women are most likely to suffer from pre-marriage contracts being enforced. This familiar argument has been outlined in detail elsewhere (e.g. Laufer-Ukeles 2008; Wade 2012) and so will not be developed here, save to point out that at its best it only makes the argument for not giving effect to pre-nuptial contracts where the parties are not in a reasonably equal bargaining power. Baroness Hale, dissenting in *Radmacher*, was aware of this gendered aspect of the decision

> Would any self-respecting young woman sign up to an agreement which assumed that she would be the only one who might otherwise have a claim, thus placing no limit on the claims that might be made against her, and then limited her claim to a pre-determined sum for each year of marriage regardless of the circumstances, as if her wifely services were being bought by the year? Yet that is what these precedents do. In short, there is a gender dimension to the issue which some may think ill-suited to decision by a court consisting of eight men and one woman. (para 137)

The problem is that it will be rare for the parties to be in a reasonably equal position. Pre-marriage contracts are typically used where one party is far richer than the other. Even if we look at *Radmacher* itself, a case involving two professionals, there are concerns over equality of bargaining power. There we had a case that looked unlikely to involve manipulation: the couple were both reasonably well off; it was the wife who was richer; they were well educated and experienced business people. Yet we learn:

> Although the judge was sure that the wife wanted her husband to love her for herself, the wife emphasised her father's insistence, because she felt it made her seem less insensitive to her future spouse, given that the terms excluded all his potential rights… The judge found that the husband was eager to comply because he did not want the wife to be disinherited, he wanted to marry her. (para 86)

A second argument, and this is the primary argument, is that intimate relationships are in their nature fluid. They are not predictable. Some of the writings on an ethic of care are especially helpful here. As already mentioned they have distinguished an approach based on an ethic of care and one based on an ethic of justice. Held (2006), p. 15) explains how rights are related to an ethic of justice approach: 'An ethic of justice focuses on questions of fairness, equality, individual rights, abstract principles, and the consistent application of them'. As highlighted by Sevenhuijsen (1998, p. 171): 'A decision based on the ethic of justice cannot be easily changed or modified. It tends to be made once and for all, even though conditions may change at a later date.' In effect 'rights talk' means that 'real experiences' are converted into 'empty abstractions' (Tushnet 1984, p. 1364). As Smart (2003, p. 238) puts it: 'the rights approach takes and translates personal and private matters into legal language. In so doing, it reformulates them into issues relevant to law rather than to the lives of ordinary people'.

In a pre-marriage contract the couple are seeking to set down in stone their rights and responsibilities in advance. This reflects the ethic of justice, just described. The problem is that it bears little relation to intimate life. While contracts might work well when dealing with mechanical production, intimate lives are messy and unpredictable. The sacrifices called for can be unforeseen and obligations without limit. The marriage might bring children, it might not; care of a demented parent may become a major task, it may not; a disabled child may take up all the energies of one spouse, they may not. The best laid plans for the marriage may need to be discarded at a moment's notice. To seek to tie these down at the start of the relationship in some form of 'once and for all' summation of their claims against each other ignores the realities of intimate relationships.

Crucially any attempt to set down the parties rights and responsibilities is likely to work against the interests of a partner who suffers an unexpected loss or sacrifice. That is most likely occur with one party needing to undertake care work, probably connected to a child or parent. These burdens are likely to fall on women and so enforcement of pre-nuptial agreements, is likely to work to the disadvantage of women particularly.

As caregiving's demands are difficult to predict, terms agreed on at the outset of a relationship are unlikely to compensate caregivers for lost opportunities, personal projects not undertaken, or undeveloped faculties. Lady Hale captured this well in *Radmacher v Granatino* (2010):

> Choices are often made for the sake of the overall happiness of the family. The couple may move from the city to the country; they may move to another country; they may adopt a completely different lifestyle; one of them may give up a well-paid job that she hates for the sake of a less lucrative job that she loves; one may give up a deadend job to embark upon a new course of study. These sorts of things happen all the time in a relationship. The couple will support one another while they are together. And it may generate a continued need for support once they are apart.

It may be replied that the concern about unexpected care obligations fails to reflect that in *Radmacher*, as most supporters of pre-nuptial agreements would accept, there is scope for a court to depart from an agreement which is clearly unfair as unexpected events occurred or has left a party in real need.

That is true, but it fails to meet the real concern. First, it puts the burden on the disadvantaged person to demonstrate their loss. They will need to prove that, for example, the parties had not foreseen that a disabled child will be born or that impact of child care on the wife's career. It is easy to imagine a husband arguing that inevitably people realise there is the risk of disability or that if a child is born it may not be possible for a wife to continue a career. Second, we are not dealing with a class of cases where occasionally unpredictable events occur. In intimate relationships unexpected events are common. So it seems inappropriate to start with a legal structure based on contract, but then permit departure in the event of unexpected events. Third, it is going against principle of justice to allow parties to enter a contract that departs from the approach taken by the courts that parties to a marriage must share the advantages and disadvantages that the relationship brings (Diduck 2011). Lady Hale (2011, p. 14) writing extra-judicially has pointed out that in the twentieth century the Victorian notion of freedom of contract has set aside especially in long-running relationships. She points to the extensive regulation of the employer/employee and landlord/tenant, where the scope for private ordering is very limited. She suggests that these provide a more accurate model than commercial contracts. We do not normally allow people to contract in a way which runs against principles of basic justice. Restrictions on the minimum wage; hours of employment; and credit agreements demonstrate that we accept that parties should be forbidden from entering contracts which undermine basic values we wish to uphold in our society. Discrimination law prohibits parties from entering contracts which are discriminatory. To allow a party to use a pre-marriage contract to take more than their fair share of marital property is likely to lead results that will in general discriminate against women and those involved in care work. We should as willing to give effect to contracts that deprive those who have dedicated the relationship to care work an equal share of the family's earnings, than we should allow an employer to pay men more than women performing the same job.

If the law were to accept the arguments based on autonomy in favour of enforcing pre-marriage contracts we could easily end up enforcing contracts which devalued child care. It may be the couple themselves devalue child care. We have all come across men who claim mothers have it easy just sitting around drinking tea all day; and even mothers who disparage their own role reflect the demeaning view often taken within society of child care (Deacon 2007). But that does mean the law should accept and enforce their understanding of the value of what they do. Financial orders on divorce can therefore impact on the appreciation and value attached to nurturing work (Williams 2000, pp. 124–127). As Williams (1998, p. 119) has emphasised:

> If we as a society take children's need for parental care seriously, it is time to stop marginalizing the adults who provide it.

This links to a further point and that is that public importance that are determined on the financial orders made on relationship breakdown (Herring 2005). A contract which left a woman far worse off after a marriage when she had undertaken the caring work would not just be doing a wrong to her but would be harming society. The lack of respect shown to care work and the lack of respect thereby shown to women in general would be harmful to the wider community (Silbaugh 1996). We already live in a society in which care work goes largely unrecognised and unvalued. The making of financial orders on divorce is one of the few areas in which care work is recognised (Case 2001).

If we imagined a world in which there were no financial orders available on divorce, we would thereby be creating a world in which everyone was encouraged to be financially self-sufficient. It would be a foolish parent who gave up employment to care for a child or ailing relative. They would be putting themselves at grave financial risk. If the relationship broke down they would be in a financially disadvantageous position. It would be much more sensible for them to rely on paid care for their children. There are some who would regard that as a good thing (Schultz 2000). But to many the vision of a world of mass day care, the discouragement of personal care and encouragement for financial independence is a horror. If undertaking personal care is an option that we wish to preserve we must have a system that does not render the undertaking of family care and home making financially very risky. Hale LJ (as she then was) recognised this clearly in *SRJ v DWJ (Financial Payments)* (1999):

> It is not only in [the child's] interest but in the community's interests that parents, whether mothers or fathers, and spouses, whether husbands or wives, should have a real choice between concentrating on breadwinning and concentrating on home-making and childrearing, and do not feel forced, for fear of what might happen should their marriage break down much later in life, to abandon looking after the home and the family to other people for the sake of maintaining a career.

Financial orders on divorce will reflect the norms that are said to underlie the marital relationship. The orders made can seek therefore to reinforce certain norms or to downplay others (Smith 2000, p. 215). This might be to privilege independence and autonomy or to recognise the value and vulnerability that care work gives rise to. As Regan (1999, p. 166) explains:

> The ideas of autonomy as independence and obligation as consensual rest upon the valorization of the realm of the market in which men traditionally have been the primary agents, and the marginalization of a realm in which women traditionally have been the primary actors. Relationships marked by personal dependence, vulnerability, care and affection are taken as relevant in conceptualising the fundamental terms of human interaction and in defining autonomy.

Through financial orders on divorce, determined by the values of the law, our community is able to recognise the value and importance of care work. There is much more that our society needs to do to properly value that work, but this is a starting point. Enforcing pre-marriage contracts would deprive the law of this way of acknowledging the importance of care. As Lady Hale (2011, p. 14) writes:

> it comes back to what we think marriage is and is for. Is it simply a private arrangement from which each can walk away when they want and without regard to the consequences for the other? Or is it a status in which we all have an interest? Do we want to encourage responsible families, in which people are able to compromise their place in the world outside the home for the sake of their partners, their children and their elderly or disabled relatives, and can be properly compensated for this if things go wrong? I continue to hope that we do.

There are yet further problems for the contractual model for determining the content of marital obligations. As Sanger (2006, p. 1322) notes most jurisdictions require some kind of disclosure before a marital contact is enforceable:

> And just what would full disclosure entail? Slovenly tendencies? Insights about one's constancy? Under the contractual model, disclosures would no longer go to the essence of marriage—marriage has been abolished—but to the heart or essence of each particular transaction. If one party is aware of a genetic predisposition to breast cancer or to Alzheimer's disease, must this fact be revealed?

Not only that but as the study by Baker and Emery (1993) demonstrated there is enormous optimism about marriage by those entering it.

At the heart of the problem with pre-marriage contracts is the assumption that the contract model which has worked effectively in a commercial context will operate in the context of an intimate relationship. Ellman (2011, p. 267) writes

> We take that view because the relationship between the parties to a qualifying nuptial agreement is very different from the relationship between the parties to a commercial contract. It is an emotional one as well as a financial one, and that is likely to make people behave differently. That goes for all contracts between spouses of course, and the general law of contract—in particular the law relating to duress and undue influence—addresses the emotional qualities of the relationship. But provision for future relationship breakdown takes the contract into the realms of the unknown and the unexpected. It seems likely that couples tend to enter into marital property agreements, particularly pre-nuptial agreements, with less realism, and more optimism, about the consequences of the contract than do most commercial negotiators:
>
> > Nearly all premarital agreements involve special difficulties arising from unrealistic optimism about marital success, the human tendency to treat low probabilities as zero probabilities…

Wightman (2000, p. 93) in an insightful analysis has drawn out some further points. He notes that inevitably there are "gaps" in a contract because the contract cannot cover every eventuality explicitly and terms have to be interpreted. In the commercial context there are norms built up by the contracting community (either generally or by those involved in a particular area of business) which can be drawn on to give the contract the kind of certainty it needs. However, Wightman notes, there is not equivalent source of norms for marriage or intimate relationships. Secondly that the kinds of values underpinning commercial contracts and which might be taken to form their basis have a very different from the altruistic and cooperative values of an intimate relationship. Commercial contracts can be taken to have making money are their bottom line and interpretation of the contract can be taken as that being the goal and purpose of the contract or the commercial relationship underpinning the contract. We cannot, of course, say the same for intimate relationships.

Pulling these points together, the law on obligations during marriage play an important role in ensuring care work is respected and that women are not disadvantaged through marriage. These are important principles of justice and important for social goods too. Parties should not be permitted to contract out of these benefits. As George (2012, p. 83) puts it:

> Entering a marriage is, in some ways, more like jointing a club. If you meet the entry requirement, you may become a member, but that does not entitled you to alter the club's rules unilaterally. You can join the club or not, and you an campaign to change the rules of the club whether you are a member or not but you cannot both be a member of the club and refuse to abide by its current rules.

5.2 Adolescent Medical Decision Making

The debates over the extent to which children should be able to make decisions about their medical treatment are well known and the battle lines firmly drawn (Kelly 2005; Mutcherson 2005; Herring 2013, Chap. 8). In the one corner there are the welfarists keen to protect children from harm and ensure that competent children are not denied the medical treatment they need, while also not wanting competent treatment to be able to veto the treatment that they need. In the other corner are the children's rights supporters, decrying the failure of the law to protect the autonomy rights of competent adolescents. Less prominent, at least in English writing, are yet a third group decrying the law's failure to respect the rights of parents in this area. These positions have been well documented and presented in the literature (Bridgeman 2007, Chap. 1).

What might a relational autonomy perspective add to this debate? First, it would question the separation of the interests of children and adults that all these approaches take. It is an obvious point, but one which is often overlooked, that decision about a child in, say, the health, educational or religious upbringing arena, can have huge repercussions on the lives of the parents (Herring 1997; Gilbar 2011). Medical decisions involving children rarely issues which affect only the child. Of course it is equally true that medical decisions involving adults will have a huge impact on their children and others close to them (Herring 2008). This transcends the merely practical implications of receiving or not receiving a treatment. In one of the best discussions on this issue Bridgeman (1998, pp. 112–113) writes:

> rather than attempt to articulate justice and provide explanations for forced treatment in terms of the rights of the abstract autonomous individual of liberal legal theory or the paternalistic overriding of those rights, it would be instructive to listen to the parents of sick children, heath care professionals and lawyers acting in partnership in order to secure the well-being of the child. If the 'different voice' can be heard in what they say, decisions relating to the medical treatment of children may be more convincingly explained in terms of the responsibility of caring than presently achieved with expressions of autonomy. What we hear may enable us to develop, out of the vague best interests test, an ethic of care model for health care decision in relation to children which explains why, because we care, sometimes medial treatment may be imposed upon them despite their wishes to the contrary.

It is, therefore, not a straight-forward matter of deciding what is best for the child or what the child's rights require. All the family member's interests are involved and the issue cannot be reduced to a matter simply concerning the legal response to one family member.

Second, as argued above our vision of autonomy presupposes a competent, independent strong adult making choices for themselves. Children, it is commonly argued lack the independence, competence and experience that adults have and so are not entitled to make decisions for themselves. Yet are not adults too vulnerable and open to abuse? Are not adults dependent on others to pursue their vision of a good life and dependent on the cooperation of others to pursue their goals? Are not adults all too often lacking the necessary knowledge and experience to make important children? Adults are in many ways as vulnerable, dependent on others and lacking in competence as children. The difficulties that many have in granting adult rights to children in the medical arena have as much to say about our puffed up vision of ourselves as adults as it does about the true vulnerability of children. A vision of autonomy that respecting and promoted relationships and saw individuals as interconnected to others would be more appropriate for not only children but adults too (Herring 2004).

Hence it is that despite its influence and sophistication there is something troubling about Michael Freeman (1997, p. 38)'s vision of children's rights which is based on the suggestion that:

> [t]he question we should ask ourselves is: what sort of action or conduct would we wish, as children to be shielded against on the assumption that we would want to mature to a rationally autonomous adulthood and be capable of deciding on our own system of ends as free and rational beings?

Such an approach promotes rational autonomy as the ideal for our children on the brink of adulthood. While placing children at the age of 18 with the maximum chance of autonomy is a laudable goal, it should not be the only one. Do we also not want children who care, understand their responsibilities, know how to develop relationships; know how not to insist on having their way? This may mean not respecting a child's autonomy interests to the extent Freeman might wish. In relationships of care we do not always get our own way. Sometimes this will mean occasionally that even competent children's wishes in relation to medical treatment will not be followed. Indeed, adults' decisions too in respect of their medical treatment should not always be followed. There are times, be we adults or children, where our relational obligations require a limit upon our right to refuse medical treatment.

Cockburn (2005, p. 72) argues:

> If…one looks at the relationship between mother and child, we see human reciprocity based on characteristics of nurturing and dependence, rather than competition and autonomy. In the case of the mother–child relationship, mutual respect and equality of worth are of more importance than any contractarian principles based on equal legal rights. The moral repertoire also needs to include principles of cooperation, intimacy, trust, connection and compassion to be emphasized as important sources of moral reasoning.

These values should underpin the legal reasoning in these medical cases too. As Bridgeman (2007, Chap. 2) emphasises reaching solutions to these troublesome cases requires a careful attention to the individual relationships concerned and the responsibilities that arise from them. This means that it is not possible to produce a single clear rule to apply in these cases, rather the solution is to be fashioned from the relationships themselves. Because whatever else happens in these medical decisions, the child and her carers will need to continue in their relationships together and those relationships are worth more than any abstract legal rights.

This discussion shows how individual autonomy fails to work for children, just as it does for adults (Foster 2009). Similarly the proxy for individual autonomy, best interests of the child, suffers likewise. The interests and rights of family members are intermingled and must be understood in their relational context. A solution must be found which fits in with the particular relationship of the parties involved. This does not lead to a neat legal solution, such as children over fourteen can always refuse treatment. It requires a careful analysis of the particular child and family and their relationships, if an appropriate response can be found. In the next section it will be argued that in fact the notion of children's welfare, if understood in a relational way, can be developed to take these values into account.

5.3 Relationship-Based Welfare

The Children Act 1989 opens in section 1 with one of the central principles of English family law:

When a court determines any question with respect to—

(a) the upbringing of a child; or
(b) the administration of a child's property or the application of any income arising from it
(c) the child's welfare shall be the court's paramount consideration.

When a judge is considering what is in the welfare of the child Section 1(3) provides a checklist of factors to consider. There has considerable debate over the meaning of the word 'paramount' in section 1(1). The accepted interpretation is that it means that the welfare of child is the sole consideration.[1] The interests of adults and other children are only relevant in so far as they may impact on the welfare of the child (Herring 1999b).

In the case of adults lacking capacity, section 1(5) of the Mental Capacity Act (2005) provides:

> An act done, or decision made, under this Act for or on behalf of a person who lacks capacity must be done, or made, in his best interests.

[1] UN Convention on the Rights of Children, in article 3, states that the child's welfare should be the primary consideration. This appears to place slightly less weight on children's interests than s 1 of the Children Act 1989.

This involves a consideration of all the relevant issues to determine what will best promote their welfare. The *Mental Capacity Act: Code of Practice* (Department of Constitutional Affairs 2007: para 5.7) states:

> When working out what is in the best interests of the person who lacks capacity to make a decision or act for themselves, decision-makers must take into account all relevant factors that it would be reasonable to consider, not just those that they think are important. They must not act or make a decision based on what they would want to do if they were the person who lacked capacity.

Although a broad range of factors is to be taken into account the focus must be on the best interests of the person lacking capacity (P) and the interests of those they are in caring relationships with are not in themselves to be given any weight in the assessment (Manthorpe et al. 2007, p. 557). Section 5.4 provides factors that for a person, or court, seeking to ascertain what is in a person's best interests.

The approach under the Children Act 1989 and the Mental Capacity Act 2004 is misguided. These are based on the assumption we can separate out one person's interests from another. However, people do not understand their personal lives as involving clashes of individual rights or interests, but rather as a working through of relationships (Bridgeman 2007, Chap. 1). The muddled give and take of everyday caring life where sacrifices are made and benefits gained, without them being totted up on some giant familial star chart, chimes more with everyday life than the image of independent interests and rights (Cockburn 2005). The woman looked after her demented mother is not carefully adding up the pounds and hours to ensure her rights are protected. In relationship the interests and well-being of the two people become merged. As Diana Meyers (2004, p. 299) puts it, the self:

> is the interpersonally bounded self…As relational selves…people share in one another's joys and sorrows, give and receive care, and generally profit from the many rewards and cope with the many aggravations of friendship, family membership, religious or ethnic affiliation, and the like. These relationships are sources of moral identity, for people become committed to their intimates and to others whom they care about, and these commitments become central moral concerns.

When good things happen to those we are in caring relationships with then that is good for us. The same is true for the bad things. Hence there is the objection to the traditional approaches of the law based on seeking to protect the interests of one party or the rights of one party. That just makes no sense when lives are so intertwined and our identities so merged (Shakespeare 2000, Chap. 1). In intimate relationships, we do not break down into 'me' and 'you' (Clement 1996, p. 11). Catriona Mackenzie (2009, p. 100) writes: 'To be a person is to be a temporally extended embodied subject whose identity is constituted in and through one's lived bodily engagement with the world and others'. So, we cannot isolate the interests of a child or a person lacking from capacity from their family members.

Nevertheless, there is value in putting especial attention on the interests of children or adult family members who lack capacity. History teaches us, as do current events, how easily those who cannot stand up for themselves can have their interests downtrodden by those with more power. Recently in England the news has been replete with stories of abuse of children in homes, hospitals and community housing (e.g. Care Quality Commission 2012). Elevating the interests of the child to the paramount position in the law ensures that the most vulnerable parties to a dispute are given the highest possible level of protection. It seeks to redress the lack of respect and protection they otherwise receive in the law.

Doing so, sends an important symbolic message emphasising the value, importance and vulnerability of children. This message has significance not only for legal language, but also the wider social discourse. It encourages parents and those caring for incapacitate adults to focus on them, rather than their own rights and interests. The welfare principle and best interests approaches are particularly important in respect of legal disputes when the voices of children are rarely heard in courts (James et al. 2003). Without the statute forcing the courts' attention on them their interests could be so easily side-lined.

The argument promoted in this book is that the interests of children should be paramount, but that their interests must be understood in a relational way. Asking what is in a child's best interests, is right question. But it must be understood to ask what order will be in their best interests understood within the context of the relationships they live in. That involves looking at what has happened in the relationships to date and what will happen in the future. It will acknowledge the care work that has been provided in the past and the value of that; and In what follows I will first address the complaint that the best interests test is too indeterminate and define it from a relational perspective. I will then explain further what I mean by relational welfare.

5.3.1 Indeterminacy Concerns

Probably the most common criticism of welfare/best interests test is that its application is unpredictable (e.g. Mnookin 1975). It can be difficult enough to predict what factors the courts will weigh up, let alone predict what the result will be in the court's assessment. In *Re S (Adult Patient: Sterilisation (2001: para 30)* Thorpe LJ stated:

> in deciding what is best ... the judge must have regard to ... welfare as the paramount consideration. That embraces issues far wider than the medical. Indeed it would be undesirable and probably impossible to set bounds to what is relevant to a welfare determination.

However, that concern will count for little from a relational perspective. Indeed as suggested above, avoiding generalised approaches and finding the solution which will be appropriate in the context of the particular case at hand is very much what would be promoted by a relational approach. A good example might be the decision of the Supreme Court in *Re B (A Child) (2009)* where it was emphasised that presumption about what was normally good for children, was not helpful for a court determining what was best for this particular child. As Lord Kerr noted (at para 35) the kind of cases that come to court are rarely 'normal' and so considering what is best for this child, it is not helpful to consider what is normally best for children. The best interests test acknowledges that each child is different and lives in different networks of relationships. Presumptions or assumptions based on what is in children's welfare are not helpful in determining what is best for the particular child before the court.

It is, therefore, quite proper that the law on resolution of disputes over children has indeterminacy. That is because it seeks to fashion a response that responds to the particular child and particular family in each case. It quite properly rejects a solution that seeks to impose a "one size fits all" response on all cases.

5.3.2 Making Welfare/Best Interests Relational

The criticisms of the traditional welfare principle/best interest test from a relational perspective will be rather different. First, it imagines that we can consider the welfare/best interests of a child in isolation from those in caring relationship with her. That, of course, will be fiercely rejected by a relational approach. As argued above in intimate relationships the interests of children and those in relationship with them become intermingled.

Susan Boyd (2010, p. 2) has written powerfully of the way that the care giving of mother enables a child to become autonomous, yet the very act of care giving restricts the autonomy of mothers. This is a common feature of family life, that at different points and times in life dreams are not pursued to enable other family members to persue theirs. Boyd (2010, p. 2) believes the impact of this on women is particularly significant, arguing:

> the still powerful societal expectations that mothers will provide primary care for children, and the strong sense of responsibility that many or most mothers feel towards the well-being of their children, the constraints that parenting imposes on female autonomy remain more significant than those on male autonomy.

Second, in focusing just on children the court there is a danger of producing a result which works to the disadvantage of mothers. Orders will be made that may purport to benefit children, but severely interfere in the rights of those caring for her. Indeed one of the consequences of the individualised image of best interests is that the caring work which is essential to those best interests and relationships which are needed to support them are unrecognised. As it is most likely to be women who undertake the care work, women are disadvantaged by such an approach (Wallbank 2010).

A third concern is that welfare/best interests order often take a narrow focus on best interests. They consider what at this point in time will promote the welfare/best interests of CLC, rather than looking at the broader picture and considering the issue in the light of the whole relationship between the parties: what has gone on to date and what is likely to occur in the future. A good example can be seen in

Re S (A Child) (2002). The case involved an attempt to prevent a mother moving to Cornwall with her daughter, Victoria, who was nine and a half years old and had Downs Syndrome. Victoria had mild learning difficulties and a range of other medical problems. Her parents had separated when she was 18 months and later divorce. She lived with her mother in South London, but had weekly contact with her father, who lived nearby and had remarried. The mother had met a new partner, who lived in Cornwall. His mother was dependant on him and lived there. There was a seven hour journey. The mother wished to move to Cornwall, but the father sought an order requiring her to remain in London. The court granted the order, a decision affirmed on appeal. The key question was what was in the best interests of Victoria. The mother's strong desire to be with her new partner and the fact she had suffered depression after the initial refusal to leave London, could not be relevant factors, save as they impacted on the welfare of the child. The expert evidence showed that Victoria would find the reduction in contact with the father confusion and it would cause her distress. It was, therefore, in her welfare to remain in London.

The difficulty with this decision is that it focused entirely on what was in her welfare at that moment. It failed to look at the broader timescale. In particular the fact this was a girl with considerable needs who had been given continuous intense care by her mother and would continue to receive that level of care for the rest of her life. The sacrifices made by her mother were enormous. While the father had been free to remarry and start his new life, the mother, through this order, was being deprived of the practical and emotional day-to-day support of her new partner. It is hard to see how, looking at this issue in the context of the relationships between the parties this order promoted Victoria's welfare. It is in the nature of the relationships that there is give and take. That is what healthy relationships involve. Relationships in which one party does all the taking and none of the receiving is not beneficial. In this case allowing the move, even if that would have caused some harm, would have been productive of a beneficial on-going relationship.

Is there a way of making welfare/best interests more relational-friendly? It is argued that there is. The first point to make is that although the welfare principle or best interests test has been interpreted by the courts to mean that, the child's welfare/best interests is the sole consideration. The court will therefore pursue the course which best promotes the interests of P, regardless of the impact on the interests of others. However, in practice courts have found ways of protecting interests or parents and carers while adhering to the welfare/best interests principle (Herring 1999a). We will not go into the devices used here, but suggest the courts can be much more bold and open in doing this if they have a better understanding of welfare/best interests.

Relationship-based welfare is best promoted when they are cared for in healthy relationships (Herring 2005). Under such an approach, cases can be resolved by recognising and acting in the child's interests whilst heeding carers' interests and the integrity of the family as a whole. If carers were to take every decision for the child considering only the child's welfare, that would not in fact promote the child's welfare. None of us would wish to be raised in a way that placed enormous burdens on our carers in order to promote our welfare, maybe just the tiniest bit. We would accept that decision might be made which on a particular occasion were not in our best interests, but which were part of a fair give and take in the relationships. Relationship-based welfare provides a means of holding onto the welfare or best interests principle while respecting the rights and interests of caregivers.

One criticism of this approach is that there is a need to adopt a 'more detached view' of child's interests in order that they are centralised and not side-lined by those of others (Eekelaar 2002). However, to see child's interests outside their relationship with their carers could be said to be artificial and as excluding much of what is of value to the child. Similarly, to view the interests of the carer without accounting for the interests of child is to exclude many important issues. Relationship-based welfare/best interests allows for a clear focus on the child's past, on-going and future relationships.

The decision of *Re Y (Mental Patient: Bone Marrow Donation) (1997)* provides an interesting a revealing example of how the best interests test operates, but a relational approach would work better. A 25 year old woman (Y) lacked capacity and lived in a community home, where she was regularly visited by her mother. Y's sister suffered from a bone disorder and her only prospect of a recovery was if a bone marrow donor could be found. The only suitable donor who could be found was Y. The sister sought a declaration that the harvesting of Y's bone marrow be authorised. Connell J granted the declaration. The donation would be in Y's best interests. The reasoning is revealing. It was explained that Y's mother was very important to Y's welfare. Y was anxious due to the sister's illness. If the sister died this would have a severe impact on the mother's health and this would, in turn, impact on Y's welfare. It was, therefore, in Y's welfare to donate the marrow. The physical discomfort and invasion caused by the donation were outweighed by the emotion and psychological benefits. My argument will be not that the result reached was incorrect, but that the reasoning is weak. The same reasoning could be used if Y's sister needed cosmetic surgery and that using tissue from Y would help the surgery go well, if that gave the mother pleasure. To exclude from the reasoning the fact that a life would be saved seems to ignore the elephant in the room.

A relational best interest approach would look at the relationships between Y, her mother and sister and the responsibilities that arose from those relationships. More might need to be known about the details of these relationships to fully analyse the situation. However, it is quite possible that the same result would be reached. But the reasoning would not be based on the benefits to Y of keeping her mother happy, but rather based on the responsibilities flowing from the relationship between her and her family.

A relational approach to best interests/welfare can also be supported through an examination of the philosophical literature on best interests/well-being. Charles Foster and Herring (2012) argued that a proper understanding of a person's wellbeing can require decisions to be made which will primarily benefit (or appear primarily to benefit) another person. That is because a 'good life' is not just about promoting one's own happiness. A good life is one that involves the cultivation of virtues; deep relationships with others; and a meeting of one's responsibilities.

There is an obvious and strong objection to our view. Is it virtuous to have a virtuous decision made on your behalf? Does compelled altruism lose the moral virtue of altruism? The very fact one is incapable of making decisions for oneself might be thought to indicate that one has been robbed of the chance to be virtuous or meet one's responsibilities. Some will say that this argument cannot apply to an adult who permanently lacks capacity and can never hope to develop virtue. I disagree. I would question the assumption that children or adults lacking capacity cannot be virtuous because they lack the capacity to choose. Choice, it is commonly assumed, is central to the notion of a virtue. But can we say that children and those lacking mental capacity are incapable of being virtuous? No. There are two reasons why not.

First, it embodies an unduly narrow understanding of virtue. Virtues are not an expression of rational choice. Anyone dealing with those lacking mental capacity knows that they rarely lack desires, attitudes, sensibilities or expectations, that can form the basis of a virtue. In these, and in their cultivation, virtue can be found. The toddler who cuddles the crying friend exhibits compassion and empathy, even if they lack the mental capacity to express it in those terms. The love and care exhibited there is a simple expression of feeling. Those without mental capacity are perfectly capable of expressing warmth, affection and kindness, even if they lack the capacity to articulate what they are doing.

Secondly, our assumption that 'we' (the capacitous adults) have the autonomy and strength to be virtuous, while 'they' (the children and those lacking capacity) do not, involves not only, a misunderstanding of virtue, but also involves an inaccurately inflated view of ourselves. We might like to pretend we are autonomous and strong (Herring 2012). The reality is a little less grand. The exhausted carer returning the demented adult to bed in the early hours of the morning, may not be exercising rational capacity but are certainly showing capacity. Many of our virtuous activities are not a reflection of rational capacity, at least not primarily so.

If then we understand welfare/best interests in a broad sense as involving the cultivation of virtue, developing relationships and the meeting of responsibilities; and we understand that we cannot but consider the relationships a person is in the health of these if we wish to promote their welfare, does this meet the needs of relational theorists. I would argue that to a large extent it does. There will be some theoretical quibbles: even this relationship-based welfare model might not capture the intermingling of the self the relational ethicist would see. There may be concerns that while with a sophisticated understanding of welfare the relational issues can be taken on board, we cannot be sure that a more simplistic version of welfare will be used. Nevertheless it has been shown that a sensitive use of the welfare/best interests can capture many of the issues that concern a relational theorist.

In Smart and Neale (1998, p. 192) insightful analysis of welfare they promote the idea that the law should focus on actuality (looking at the real practical needs and wishes of children, including who has been the primary carer and whether or not there has been a climate of fear); the principle of care (placing the child within the context of the relationships she lives in; including the need for parents to be cared for); the principle of recognition of selfhood (recognising that parents mothers have an interest in their autonomy) and the principle of recognition of loss (a realisation that parties may have suffered loss). All of these can readily be taken into account in the context of relational welfare (Rhoades 2010).

5.4 Domestic Abuse

Turning, finally, to the issue of domestic abuse. It is suggested that a relational autonomy perspective offers some important insights into the issue. First, a relational perspective gives us a better understanding of what domestic abuse is. Second, it helps explain why ensuring there is an effective legal response to domestic abuse is so important. Third, it helps analyse the weight that should be attached to the wishes of the victim in a case of domestic abuse who opposes legal intervention.

5.4.1 The Wrong of Domestic Violence

If autonomy is about developing and living out a vision for one's own flourishing, for many, if not all, that involves being in relationships with others. As seen earlier, many regard the primary role of the state must be to refrain from intervention in the intimate aspects of life. The best way for love to flourish and the relationship to grow is for the state to keep well out. John Eekelaar (2007, p. 82) has supported a very moderate version of this argument, calling for respect of the intimate sphere. We need to respect 'the value of having space to develop one's personality and personal interaction free from external gaze…love itself demands such a space if it is to sustain a lifelong partnership'. However, his view is significantly tempered by his later (at 78) emphasis that although the personal sphere if privileged, it is not 'licensed for irresponsibility' and 'respect for the privileged sphere may …demand intervention where harm is inflicted within it'.

Of course not all relationships are good. Relationships and social structures can be oppressive. A central aspect of relational approaches must be in protecting people from the harms that abusive relationships can cause. A relational approach should not seek to support all relationships. It is here that there is likely to be disagreement among relational ethicists. Care ethicists would seek to promote relationships marked by mutual care and respect. Other relational ethicists might emphasise the role of autonomy: we should protect those relationships that a person has chosen to enter into. Whichever is taken, if the law seeks to promote relationships, it must make sure those are a safe place to be.

Academics and courts have struggled to agree on domestic violence. That is not surprising it is a complex phenomena and is the is a spectrum of behaviour which could be classified as domestic abuse. What, it is suggested, may be more helpful is to identify what it is about domestic abuse which makes it particularly wrongful. Even if we cannot draw a bright line over what is or is not domestic abuse, we can identify characteristics that mark the abuse as wrongful. Relational perspectives provide a particularly helpful way of doing this (Herring 2011; Madden Dempsey 2006). The following three features are central to the notion of domestic abuse.

First, domestic abuse should be understood as a programme of "coercive control" to use the phrase of Evan Stark (2007). We need to understand an incident of abuse within its broader relational context. Criminal law traditionally does not do this. It considers the severity of the injury, but not its broader context. The problem with such an approach, especially in the context of emotional abuse is well demonstrated by the English case of R v Dhaliwal [2006] EWCA Crim 1139, in which it was found a husband who reduced his wife to an 'emotional wreck', through an on-going regime of emotional abuse. The wife committee suicide. His prosecution for her manslaughter failed because it could not be proved that any one incident was sufficiently serious to amount to a criminal offence. This reveals the law's inability to consider the broader context and impact of acts, and over-emphasis on bodily injury. The reality of what the husband had done to the wife could only be understood by looking at the whole nature of the relationship between them and understand what had happened from her perspective (Burton 2010).

Listening to the victims of domestic abuse it is clear that the impact is in terms of the overall controlling nature of the relationships. It is a program of 'coercive control' (to use Evan Stark's (2007) phrase) or 'patriarchal terrorism' or 'intimate terrorism' (to use Michael Johnson's (2005) phrase), rather than a series of individual incidents. Michael Johnson distinguishes intimate terrorism from what he calls 'situational couple violence' or 'mutual violence'. Patriarchal terrorism is 'violence enacted in the service of taking general control over one's partner' Johnson (2005, p. 35). Situational couple violence, by contrast, does not involve an attempt the control the relationship. Rather the relationship is generally marked by equality, but there is one off incident of violence, perhaps, a lashing out in self-defence, anger or frustration.

Mary Ann Dutton, a psychologist, (Dutton 2003, p. 1204) explains:

> Abusive behaviour does not occur as a series of discrete events. Although a set of discrete abusive incidents can typically be identified within an abusive relationship, an understanding of the dynamic of power and control within an intimate relationship goes beyond these discrete incidents. To negate the impact of the time period between discrete episodes of serious violence—a time period during which the woman may never know when the next incident will occur, and may continue to live with on-going psychological abuse—is to fail to recognize what some battered woman experience as a continuing 'state of siege'.

The kind of control which is involved is designed to isolate the victim, form her friends and limit independence, by, for example, restricting access to work. Physical violence is only one tool that may be used to do this (Rachmilovitz 2007,

p. 496). Undermining of self-confidence and self-worth through emotional abuse is another way of doing it. Incidents which might appear trivial can be seen as having a significant impact when appreciated in their broader context (Burke 2007, p. 552).

A second aspect of the wrong of domestic abuse is that it involves a breach of trust. Intimate relationships involves 'thick interpersonal trust' (Khodyakov 2007, p. 117). In them secrets are laid bare and knowledge gained which will be known by no one else. Honesty and vulnerability are essential to a close relationship. John Eekelaar (2007, pp. 4–47) has argued that trust is at the heart of the intimacy, and that enables love and autonomy to develop. That trust, however, creates obligations, not to misuse the information learned during the relationship or to take advantage of the vulnerability inevitably created by intimacy. Yet that is precisely what domestic abuse does.

And it does so in a particular painful way. Our intimate relationships should help form our identity; give us a sense of self-worth; add values to our lives (Rachmilovitz 2007). Domestic abuse uses those relationships to do the opposite: to destroy our identity; to destroy self-worth and rob life of its value. As Stark (2007, p. 363) writes:

> In the romantic vernacular, love and intimacy compensate women for their devaluation in the wider world. Personal life does something more. It provides the state where women practice their basic rights, garner the support needed to resist devaluation, experiment with sexual identities, and imagine themselves through various life projects. Coercive control subverts this process, bringing discrimination home by reducing the discretion in everyday routines to near zero, freezing feeling and identity in time and space, the process victims experience as entrapment. Extended across the range of activities that define women as persons, this foreshortening of subjective development compounds the particular liberty harms caused by coercive control.

Third, the impact of domestic abuse does not simply affect the couple, it impacts upon and is reinforced by, broader social attitudes. As the Parliamentary Assembly, Council of Europe, Committee on Equal Opportunities for Women and Men (2002: para 12) puts it:

> Violence against women is a question of power, of the need to dominate and control. This in turn is rooted in the organization of society, itself based on inequality between the sexes. The meaning of this violence is clear: it is an attempt to maintain the unequal relationship between men and women and to perpetuate the subordination of women.

Domestic abuse relies upon and reinforces inequalities that exist within society. For example, the attempts by the male perpetrators of abuse to prevent their female partners entering the workplace or public arena are but imitations of broader restrictions women face in accessing the workplace. Madden Dempsey (2007, p. 938) explains:

> the patriarchal character of individual relationships cannot subsist without those relationships being situated within a broader patriarchal social structure. Patriarchy is, by its nature, a social structure—and thus any particular instance of patriarchy takes its substance and meaning from that social context. If patriarchy were entirely eliminated from society, then patriarchy would not exist in domestic arrangements and thus domestic

> violence in its strong sense would not exist… Moreover, if patriarchy were lessened in society generally then ceteris paribus patriarchy would be lessened in domestic relationships as well, thereby directly contributing to the project of ending domestic violence in its strong sense.

This is a specific example of the broader point that what happens in intimate relationships does impact upon society more broadly. In the UK (Home Office 2011, p. 2) indicate that 29 % of women have experienced domestic abuse since they were 16. 54 % of serious sexual assaults were by a current or former partner. And it starts at a young age. A recent survey found that 16 % of teenage girls questioned (whose average age was 15) had been hit by their boyfriends. A further 15 % had been pushed and 6 % forced to have sex by their boyfriends (NSPCC 2005, p. 1). Clearly the impact are of broader significance.

While supporters of relational autonomy often emphasise the value of relationships, they must also be alert to relationships which prevent a person living out their life as they wish. It we are to promote and enable good relationships, we must at the same time recognise that those entering intimate relationships make themselves vulnerable to abuse. Without an effective legal regime of protection, people will be deterred from entering intimate relationships.

5.4.2 Autonomy and Domestic Abuse

Feminists have divided over the correct response to domestic abuse cases where the victim does not want intervention (Contrast Suk 2009; Madden Dempsey 2009). Should a criminal prosecution of an abuser take place if the victim refuses? For Suk (2009) policies which seek to take an aggressive stand against domestic abuse (by having mandatory arrest, no-drop prosecution, and no-contact-order policies (see Dutton and Goodman 2006)) are in fact working against women's autonomy interests. She argues that create "state imposed de factor divorce" and such policies shift "the decision to exclude an alleged abuser away from the victim and to the state." That view is rejected here. Suk's analysis does raise some genuine issues which space prevents a discussion: about how one can prove the abuse, without the evidence of the victim; and the socio-ethnic demographic of prosecutions for domestic abuse. Instead I want to look at the commonly raised argument that the law should reflect victim's autonomous wishes and if she does not want a prosecution that wish should be respected.

Eva Feder Kittay (2007, p. 469) has argued that one must always "construe oneself and other as selves that are always selves-in-relationship". But as she recognises there is a difficulty in balancing the need to retain the worth of individuals, with the values of relationships. She argues (at 494):

> Total self-sacrifice, the annihilation of the self in favor of the cared for, is neither demanded by the practice of care nor is it justifiable, for one can see that a relationship requires two selves, not one self in which the other is subsumed and consumed. A care

> ethic is not a mere reaction to individualism, but it tempers individualism by insisting that the relationships in which we stand help to constitute the individual we have become, are now and will be in the future.

It is with this in mind that her references to understanding people as 'selves in relationship' is particularly valuable. As Frazer and Lacey (1993, p. 178) argue:

> The notion of the relational self, in contrast to both atomistic and inter-subjective selves, nicely captures our empirical and logical interdependence and the centrality to our identity of our relations with others and with practices and institutions, whilst retaining an idea of human uniqueness and discreteness as central to our sense of ourselves. It entails the collapse of any self/other or individual/community dichotomy without abandoning the idea of genuine agency and subjectivity.

Another aspect of the autonomy argument that is raised in this context is to ask why did the woman not leave the relationships if she did not wish to be part of it. Nedelsky (2012, p. 312) summarises the substantial literature on this:

> [A]busive relationships [are] in part caused by the many layers of difficulty of getting out of them: the autonomy-impairing fear and dependency created by the relationship itself; the difficulty of supporting one's kids once one has left; and the increased danger of getting killed, a danger police are not good at preventing.

As Nedlseky indicates the factors that are at play in cases involving domestic abuse are not restricted to individual psychology. A host of structures and social factors impact on the decision to enter a relationship and the power structure within it. It is not simply a matter of choice as individualistic autonomy would put it.

First, we need to be more precise about what autonomy means in this context. Coggon (2007, p. 235) has listed three versions of autonomy:

1. Ideal desire autonomy—leads to an action decided upon because it reflects what a person should want, measured by reference to some purportedly universal or objective standard of values.
2. Best desire autonomy—leads to an action decided upon because it reflects a person's overall desire given his own values, even if this runs contrary to his immediate desire.
3. Current desire autonomy—leads to an action decided upon because it reflects a person's immediate inclinations, i.e. what he thinks he wants in a given moment without further reflection.

As will immediately be apparent, a person's expressed wishes may not reflect their deeper autonomy (Walter and Ross 2013). It may reflect an immediate desire, and not a settled decision. A relational approach to autonomy adds further insight. Mackenzie and Rogers (2013), pp. 37–67) argue to be able to exercise autonomy we need to be following:

- Self-determining: being "able to determine one's own beliefs, values, goals and wants, and to make choices regarding matters of practical import to one's life free from undue interference. The obverse of self-determination is determination by other persons, or by external forces or constraints."

- Self-governing: being be able to make choices and enact decisions that express, or are consistent with, one's values, beliefs and commitments. Whereas the threats to self-determination are typically external, the threats to self-governance are typically internal, and often involve volitional or cognitive failings. Weakness of will and failures of self-control are common volitional failings that interfere with self-governance."
- Having authenticity: "a person's decisions, values, beliefs and commitments must be her 'own' in some relevant sense; that is, she must identify herself with them and they must cohere with her 'practical identity', her sense of who she is and what matters to her. Actions or decisions that a person feels were foisted on her, which do not cohere with her sense of herself, or from which she feels alienated, are not autonomous."

The notions of self-governance, self-determination and authenticity, require relationships to enable people to exercise these. However, relationships can undermine these values as much as enhance them. Domestic abuse, as we have seen, specifically works against these values. Low self-esteem; dependence upon the perpetrator; feelings of hopelessness about ending the violence; and a tendency to minimise or deny the violence are all commonly found among victims of domestic violence (Jacobson and Gottman 2007). A victim of domestic abuse, requires protection from these to enable her to achieve autonomy. Indeed it is a cruel irony that autonomy is used to leave a victim in the very relationship which undermines her autonomy.

Even putting that argument to one side, many victims if they are opposing intervention have conflicting wishes (Itzen et al. (2010)). They want to remain in the relationship, but they want the abuse to stop. In such a case it is not easy to determine what is promoting their autonomy. It is not possible to respect these two conflicting desires. I suggest that where the abuse is low level, the infringement on autonomy in remaining in the relationship will be limited. However, in more serious cases the autonomy arguments will be in favour of removal.

Third, there are strong state reasons which can justify prosecuting a case of domestic violence, even where the victim does not want intervention. There are the interests of the community is expressing a clear message that domestic violence is unacceptable and will be taken very seriously by the state (Madden Dempsey 2009). It is important to remember that prosecutions are brought by the state and not the victim. Battering can be seen as causing public harm: it can cause increased costs to the state; extensive loss to the economy of police time, victims having to take time off work, etc.

Fourth, even if these arguments are not accepted, the issue cannot be categorised as private where children are involved (Hester et al. 2007). The harms to children who witness domestic abuse are well documented (Hester et al. 2007; Tuerkheimer 2004). In such cases a simple appeal to the wishes of the victim of abuse not to be protected does not supply sufficient reason to fail to provide legal protection.

To conclude, a relational autonomy approach to domestic abuse provides a helpful insight into the nature of the phenomenon. It is not a series of discrete acts of violence, but a relationship marked by coercion and control. This enables us to appreciate why domestic abuse is such a serious wrong, requiring legal intervention. Further, that helps justify why legal protection may be required even in cases where the victim is wishing the state to stay away. Her autonomy is severely impaired and she needs to be liberated to enable her to find her autonomy again.

References

Baker L, Emery R (1993) When every relationship is above average: perceptions and expectations of divorce at time of marriage. Law Hum Behav 17: 439–578

Boyd S (2010) Autonomy for mothers? Relational theory and parenting apart. Feminist Legal Stud 18:137–158

Bridgeman J (1998) Because we care? The medical treatment of children. In: Sheldon S, Thomson M (eds) Feminist perspectives on health care. Cavendish, London p, pp 97–113

Bridgeman J (2007) Parents, young children and healthcare law. Cambridge University Press, Cambridge

Burke A (2007) Domestic violence as a crime of pattern and intent. George Wash Law Rev 75:552–593

Burton M (2010) R v Dhaliwal commentary. In: Hunter R, McGlynn C, Rackley E (eds) Feminist judgments. Hart, Oxford

Care Quality Commission (2012) Our market report. Care Quality Commission, London

Case M (2001) How high the apple pie? A few troubling questions about where, why, and how the burden of care for children should be shifted. Chicago-Kent Law Review 78:1753–1786

Clement G (1996) Care, autonomy and justice: feminism and the ethic of care. Westview, Boulder CA

Cockburn T (2005) Children and the feminist ethic of care. Childhood 12:71–89

Coggon J (2007) Varied and principled understandings of autonomy in English law: justifiable inconsistency or blinkered moralism? Health Care Anal 15:235–255

Cretney S (2003) Private ordering and divorce—how far can we go. Family Law 33:399–405

Deacon A (2007) Civic labour or doulia? Care, reciprocity and welfare. Soc Policy Soc 6:481–501

Deech R (1977) The principles of maintenance. Family Law 7:229–235

Department of Constitutional Affairs (2007) Mental Capacity Act: Code of Practice. The Stationery Office, London

Diduck A (2011) What is family law for? Curr Leg Probl 64:287–314

Dutton MA (2003) Understanding women's response to domestic violence. Hofstra Law Rev 21:1191–1212

Dutton MA, Goodman L (2006) Development and validation of a coercive control measure for intimate partner violence. US Department of Justice, Washington

Eekelaar J (2002) Beyond the welfare principle. Child and Family Law Quarterly 14:237–253

Eekelaar J (2007) Family law and personal life. Oxford University Press, Oxford

Ellman I (2011) United States. In: Scherpe J (ed) Marital agreements and private autonomy in comparative perspective. Hart Publishing, Oxford

Feder Kittay E (2007) Searching for an overlapping consensus: a secular care ethics feminist responds to religious feminists. Univ St Thomas Law J 4:468–488

Fineman M (2004) The autonomy muth. A theory of dependency. The New Press, New York

Foster C (2009) Choosing life, choosing death: the tyranny of autonomy. Hart Publishing, Oxford

Frazer E, Lacey N (1993) The politics of community: a feminist critique of the liberal communitarian debate. Harvester Wheatsheaf, Hemel Hempstead

Freeman M (1997) The moral status of children. Martinus Nijhoff, London
Gilbar R (2011) Family involvement, independence, and patient autonomy in practice. Med Law Rev 19:192–234
Hale B (2011) Equality and autonomy in family law. J Soc Welf Family Law 33:3–14
Held V (2006) The ethics of care. Oxford University Press, Oxford
Herring J (1997) Children's abortion rights. Medical Law Review 5:257–276
Herring J (1999a) The welfare principle and the rights of parents. In: Bainham A, Lindley B, Richards M (eds) What is a parent?. Hart Publishing, Oxford
Herring J (1999b) The Human Rights Act and the welfare principle—conflicting or complimentary? Child Family Law Q 11:223–235
Herring J (2004) Children's rights for grown-ups. In: Fredman S, Spencer S (eds) Age as an equality issue. Hart publishing, Oxford, pp 145–172
Herring J (2005) Farewell welfare? J Soc Welf Family Law 27:159–172
Herring J (2008) The place of carers. In: Freeman M (ed) Law and bioethics. Oxford University Press, Oxford
Herring J (2011) The meaning of domestic violence: Yemshaw v London
Herring J (2012) Vulnerability, children and the law. In: Freeman M (ed) Law and childhood studies. Oxford University Press, Oxford
Herring J (2013) Family law, 5th edn. Pearson, Harlow
Hester M, Pearson C, Harwin N (2007) Making an impact—children and domestic violence: a reader. Jessica Kingsley, York
Itzen C, Taket A, Barter-Godfrey S (2010) Domestic and sexual violence and abuse. Routledge, Abingdon
Jacobson N, Gottman J (2007) When men batter women: new insights into ending abusive relationships. Simon & Schuster, New York
James A, James A, McNamee S (2003) Constructing children's welfare in family proceedings. Family Law 33:889–893
Johnson M (2005) Apples and oranges in child custody disputes: intimate terrorism vs. situational couple violence. J Child Custody 2:43–76
Kachroo G (2007) Mapping alimony: from status to contract and beyond. Pierce Law Rev 5:163–192
Kelly F (2005) Conceptualising the child through an ethic of care: lessons for family law. Intern J Law Context 1:375–411
Khodyakov D (2007) Trust as a process: a three dimensional approach. Sociology 41:116–132
Laufer-Ukeles P (2008) Selective recognition of gender difference in the law: revaluing the caretaker role. Harv J Law Gend 31:1–36
Mackenzie C (2009) Personal identity, narrative integration and embodiment. In: Campbell S, Meynell L, Sherwin S (eds) Embodiment and agency. Pennsylvania University Press, University Park PA
Mackenzie C, Rogers W (2013) Autonomy, vulnerability and capacity: a philosophical appraisal of the Mental Capacity Act. Intern J Law Context 9:37–67
Madden Dempsey M (2006) What counts as domestic violence. William and Mary J Women Law 13:301–333
Madden Dempsey M (2007) Towards a feminist state. Mod Law Rev 70:908–935
Madden Dempsey M (2009) Prosecuting domestic violence. Oxford University Press, Oxford
Manthorpe J, Rapaport J, Stanley N (2007) Who decides now? Protecting and empowering vulnerable adults. Br J Soc Work 37:557–576
Morley J (2006) Enforceable prenuptial agreements: their time has come. Family Law 36:772
Mnookin F (1975) Child-custody adjudication: judicial functions in the face of indeterminacy. Law and Contemporary Problems 39:259–312
Mutcherson K (2005) Whose body is it anyway? An updated model of healthcare decision-making rights for adolescents. Cornell J Law Public Policy 14:251–272
Nedelsky J (2012) Law's relations. Oxford University Press, Oxford
NSPCC (2005) Teen abuse survey of Great Britain. NSPCC, London

Office Home (2011) Homicides, firearm offences and intimate violence 2009/10. Home Office, London
Parliamentary Assembly, Council of Europe, Committee on Equal Opportunities for Women and Men (2002) Domestic Violence. Council of Europe, Brussels
Rachmilovitz O (2007) Bringing down the bedroom walls: emphasizing substance over form in personalized abuse. William and Mary J Women Law 14:495–522
Rhoades H (2010) Revising Australia's parenting laws: a plea for a relational approach to children's best interests. Child Fam Law Q 23:172–194
Sanger C (2006) A case for civil marriage. Cardozo Law Rev 27:1311–1323
Schultz V (2000) Life's work. Columbia Law Rev 100:1881–1921
Sevenhuijsen S (1998) Citizenship and the ethics of care: feminist considerations about justice. Morality and Politics, Routledge, Abingdon
Shakespeare T (2000) Help. Venture, London
Silbaugh K (1996) Turning labor into love: housework and the law. Northwest Univ Law Rev 91:27–56
Singer J (1992) The privatization of family law. Wis Law Rev 5:1443–1567
Smart C (2003) Children and the transformation of family law. In: Dewar J, Parker S (eds) Family law processes, practices, pressures. Hart Publishing, Oxford, pp 238–239
Smart C, Neale B (1998) Family fragments. Policy Press, Bristol
Smith C (2000) Philosophical models of marriage and their influence on property division methods at divorce. J Contemp Leg Issues 214
Stark E (2007) Coercive control. Oxford University Press, New York
Suk J (2009) At home in the law: How the domestic violence revolution is transforming privacy. Yale University Press, New Haven
Tietjens Meyers D (2004) Narrative and moral life. In: Calhoun C (ed) Setting the moral compass. Oxford University Press, Oxford
Tuerkheimer D (2004) Recognizing and remedying the harm of battering. J Crim Law Criminol 959–1034
Tushnet M (1984) A critique of rights. Tex Law Rev 1363, 1364–1395
Wade J (2012) The perils of prenuptial financial agreements in Australia: Effectiveness and professional negligence. Law papers. Paper 425
Wallbank J (2010) '(En)Gendering the fusion of rights and responsibilities in the law of contact. In: Wallbank J, Choudhry S, Herring, J (eds), Rights, gender and family law. Routledge, Abingdon
Walter JK, Ross LF (2013) Relational autonomy as the key to effective behavioral change. Philos Psychiatry Psychol 20:169–177
Wightman J (2000) Intimate relationships, relational contract theory, and the reach of contract. Fem Leg Stud 8: 93–131
Williams J (1998) Towards a reconstructive feminism: reconstructing the relationship of market work and family work. North Ill Univ Law Rev 19:119–132
Williams J (2000) Unbending gender. Oxford University Press, New York

Cases

Radmacher v Granatino [2010] UKSC 42
Regan M (1999) Alone Together: Law and the Meaning of Marriage. Oxford University Press, New York

Legislation

Mental Capacity Act 2005

Chapter 6
Conclusion

This book has examined the concept of autonomy in family law. It has argued that traditional understandings of autonomy are based on an individualistic model which understands autonomy about a single person pursuing their own vision of the good life. This understanding of autonomy has come to play an increasingly important role in family law in recent years. Moves towards no fault divorce and the greater use of mediation are commonly justified by autonomy-based articles.

This book has argued that the use of individualistic conceptions of autonomy are inappropriate for use in family law. In fact, our understandings of ourselves is intertwined with others. We understand our intimate lives as not involving clashes of autonomy but regularly setting aside our own interests to pursue the good of those we are in relationships. Typically in health relationships this involves give and take, with some decisions being taken in line with one members views and sometimes in line with another. This is inherent within relationships and helps to produce healthy relationships which are central to most people's broad autonomous wishes.

This article has promoted the use of relational autonomy. This argues that we are in our nature relational beings. Our understanding of our selves, our identities and our plans of our lives are integrated within our relationships. It, therefore, makes no sense to talk of "my goals" in isolation for others. We need a model of autonomy which is built around the support of relationships. As Scheininger (1998, p. 283) puts it:

> Because the law is conceived of in its application to the isolated individual rather than in its application to the individual's various associations and relationships, the law does not accurately reflect the reality of human existence. The legitimacy of the law is thus challenged. Individual persons do not operate as independent, separate entities, but as interdependent, connected parts of larger groups. In failing to deal with laws as they affect human relationships, lawmakers ignore a fundamental aspect of our humanity....

Applying this to family law, we need a law which fosters relationships; which acknowledges that relationships, especially relationships of care, are essential to our societal well-being; and protects people from the disadvantages that flow from

J. Herring, *Relational Autonomy and Family Law*, SpringerBriefs in Law,
DOI: 10.1007/978-3-319-04987-8_6, © The Author(s) 2014

relationships. Applying this approach to some particular issues in family law this book has argued that we should be sceptical of pre-marriage contracts because we parties cannot predict in advance how the benefits and disadvantages which are part of a relationships will play out. Parties should not be allowed to contract so that there is not an equal sharing of the gains and losses of the relationship because doing so allows one person to take advantage of the benefits of the relationship, while not taking on its obligations. It has also been argued that in relation to medical decision making by adolescents we should acknowledge that the interests of parents and children are intertwined and this issue should not be reduced to choice between deciding whether the child or adult decides what medical treatment should be provided. Instead we need a response which is sensitive to the particular child and relational context.

The issue of the welfare/best interests test, used to resolve disputes over children. This is commonly presented as requiring the court to determine what is in the best interests of the child, without paying attention to the interests of the adults. This, it is argued, is based on a misconception. We cannot consider the interests of the child in isolation. We must understand the well-being of the child within the context of her relationships. The relationship between the child and those caring for her are essential to her well-being. We need therefore to find a relational welfare approach which seeks to ensure good relationships between a child and those caring for her. That may mean that a particular decision, seen in isolation, will not promote a child's wellbeing, but be correct if seen as an appropriate decision within the overall context of the relationship.

Finally this book has argued that a relational approach is invaluable in determining the appropriate response to domestic abuse. It helps to clarify what is the wrong which is the heart of domestic abuse: the relationships of manipulation and control by one party of another. It also helps explain why an intervention is justified, even where the victim of the abuse is not seeking official protection.

Relational autonomy provides an important tool of analysis in family law. It recognises and accepts that we have choice, but that these choices must be understood within the context of our relationships. For it is our relationships with our children; our lovers; those we care for and those who are for us who make us who we are. Few people, if any, life the atomistic ideal presumed by traditional conceptions of autonomy. We do not need a family law that liberates us to be free to peruse our goals of a good life. We need a family law that nourishes, protects and enhances the relationships that central to our lives.

Reference

Scheininger P (1998) Legal separateness, private connectedness: an impediment to gender equality in the family. Columbia J Law Soc Prob 31:283–313

FSC
www.fsc.org
MIX
Papier aus verantwortungsvollen Quellen
Paper from responsible sources
FSC® C105338

If you have any concerns about our products,
you can contact us on
ProductSafety@springernature.com

In case Publisher is established outside the EU,
the EU authorized representative is:
Springer Nature Customer Service Center GmbH
Europaplatz 3, 69115 Heidelberg, Germany

Printed by Libri Plureos GmbH
in Hamburg, Germany